Ethics and Risk Management in Online and Distance Behavioral Health

Ethics and Risk Management in Online and Distance Behavioral Health

Frederic G. Reamer
Rhode Island College

cognella®
SAN DIEGO

Bassim Hamadeh, CEO and Publisher
Amy Smith, Senior Project Editor
Abbey Hastings, Associate Production Editor
Emely Villavicencio, Senior Graphic Designer
Stephanie Kohl, Licensing Coordinator
Natalie Piccotti, Director of Marketing
Kassie Graves, Vice President of Editorial
Jamie Giganti, Director of Academic Publishing

Cover image: Copyright © 2015 iStockphoto LP/Hilch.
Copyright © 2018 iStockphoto LP/sefa ozel.

Printed in the United States of America.

Parts of this book were originally published in Frederic G. Reamer, "Clinical Social Work in a Digital Environment: Ethical and Risk Management Issues," *Theory and Practice in Clinical Social Work,* ed. Jerrold R. Brandell, pp. 649-673. Copyright © 2020 by Cognella, Inc. Reprinted with permission.

cognella® | ACADEMIC PUBLISHING

3970 Sorrento Valley Blvd., Ste. 500, San Diego, CA 92121

To Deborah, Emma, and Leah

This book includes information and commentary about legal concepts and cases. Readers who believe they need or want legal advice should consult an attorney with expertise in professional malpractice and risk management.

Contents

CHAPTER ONE

Introduction

IN THE LATE nineteenth century, when clinical psychology and social work emerged as professions, there was no in-depth discussion of professional ethics. Understandably, during those early years, practitioners focused primarily on the nature of clinical assessment, diagnosis, and treatment protocols. Certainly, practitioners of that era were cognizant of basic concepts such as client privacy, confidentiality, and self-determination, even if there was scant ethics vocabulary or conceptual frameworks in their professional armamentarium.

Over time, what are now known as behavioral health professionals—including clinical and counseling psychologists, social workers, mental health counselors, marriage and family therapists, psychiatrists, psychiatric nurses, and substance use disorder professionals—cultivated a richer, deeper, and more expansive appreciation of a wide range of ethical challenges in their work. In addition to well-known issues related to the limits of client confidentiality and self-determination, practitioners have developed values-driven, conceptually based protocols regarding informed consent, complex boundary issues, conflicts of interest, truth telling, professional paternalism, allocation of limited resources, and whistle blowing, among others.

Behavioral health pioneers certainly understood that embedded in their professions are fundamentally important and challenging moral and ethical issues. There is no question, however, that these early practitioners could not have possibly imagined some of the pressing ethical questions, conundrums, and challenges facing today's behavioral health professionals. Is it ethical for practitioners to use digital and other technology to provide services to clients they never meet in person; communicate with current or former clients on online social networking websites; exchange text messages (SMS) with clients outside of normal working hours and on practitioners' personal smartphones; provide distance or remote counseling services to clients who live outside of the jurisdiction in which the practitioner is licensed and who are located in jurisdictions in which the practitioner is not licensed; communicate with clients using encrypted smartphone apps; and search online for information about clients without their knowledge or consent?

ETHICAL CHALLENGES IN THE DIGITAL AGE

Digital technology has created unprecedented options for the delivery of behavioral health services. Increasing numbers of practitioners are relying fully or partially on various forms of digital and other technological options to serve people who are struggling with a wide range of challenges, including mood disorders, anxiety, addictions, and relationship issues. Behavioral health is no longer limited to office-based, in-person meetings with clients. Today, large numbers of practitioners are using video counseling, email chat, social networking websites, text messaging, avatar-based platforms, self-guided web-based interventions, smartphone apps, and other technology to provide services to clients, some of whom they never meet in person (Chan & Hosko, 2016; Chester & Glass, 2006; Dombo, Kays, & Weller, 2014; Kanani & Regehr, 2003; Lamendola, 2010; Menon & Miller-Cribbs, 2002; Reamer, 2012a, 2013a, 2018e; Zur, 2012).

Some behavioral health professionals are using digital technology informally as a supplement to traditional face-to-face service delivery. Other practitioners have created formal "distance" clinical practices that depend entirely on digital technology. In addition, practitioners' routine use of digital technology—especially social media and text messaging—in their daily lives has created new ways to interact and communicate with clients. These common forms of modern communication also raise ethical issues, even when practitioners do not use digital technology to provide services—such as online therapy or video counseling—per se (Campbell, Millan, & Martin, 2018; Daviss, Hanson, & Miller, 2015).

In light of these compelling developments, it is essential that behavioral health professionals address two key issues. First, practitioners must explore the ethical implications of their use of digital technology to interact with and serve clients in relatively new ways. Second, practitioners must consider whether their use of digital technology and distance counseling services alters the fundamental nature of their relationships with clients, which has traditionally entailed opportunities to develop a rich therapeutic alliance with a client in the context of ongoing face-to-face meetings (Cooper & Lesser, 2010; Reamer, 2017). Practitioners' use of digital technology poses novel challenges associated with traditional ethics concepts related to informed consent, privacy, confidentiality, professional boundaries, documentation, and client abandonment, among others.

The principal purpose of this book is to identify pertinent ethical challenges and ethically related risk-management issues that behavioral health professionals should consider if they contemplate using online and other digital technology to assist people in need. This is essential if practitioners are to protect clients from harm and prevent lawsuits and licensing board complaints associated with their use of technology and provision of services remotely. These ethical issues involve application of traditional, widely embraced, and time-honored ethics concepts in behavioral health to new challenges created by online and distance technology.

Online and distance technology in behavioral health is wide ranging. It includes the use of computers (including online chat and email) and other electronic means (such as smartphones and video technology using electronic tablets) to (a) deliver services to clients, (b) communicate with clients, (c) manage confidential case records, and (d) access information about clients (Lee, 2010; Luxton, Nelson, & Maheu, 2016; Menon & Miller-Cribbs, 2002; Reamer, 2017; Zur, 2012).

Many behavioral health professionals appreciate their ability to enhance clients' access to services using digital and other distance counseling tools and believe they can do so in a way that honors and adheres to prevailing ethical standards in behavioral health (Bashshur et al., 2016; Berle et al., 2015; Dowling & Rickwood, 2013; Mattison, 2012; Shore, 2015). They argue that distance counseling services offer a number of compelling advantages. During national health crises that limit clients' and practitioners' mobility, practitioners can use technology to serve clients without risking contagion. Also, some individuals who want social services live in remote geographic areas and would have great difficulty traveling to a practitioner's office. Clients with physical disabilities can use distance counseling options without enduring the logistical challenges and discomfort involved in arranging transportation and traveling significant distances. Individuals with overwhelming anxiety and agoraphobia can access help from home that they might not seek otherwise. People who are profoundly concerned about protecting their privacy—especially if they are well known in their local community—can receive counseling without risking exposure in a practitioner's waiting room. The around-the-clock availability of services, given the options people have to connect remotely with a practitioner somewhere in the world almost immediately any time of day or night, either online or by smartphone, also enhances practitioners' ability to help people in crisis.

Not surprisingly, many seasoned behavioral health professionals have clinical and ethical concerns about these options that facilitate remote delivery of services (Barsky, 2017, 2019; Lamendola, 2010; Mattison, 2012; Reamer, 2017; Santhiveeran, 2009). These practitioners worry that the advent and expanding use of digital and other distance service-delivery options dilutes the meaning of therapeutic relationship and alliance and compromises practitioners' ability to comply with core ethical values and standards related to informed consent, privacy, confidentiality, professional boundaries, competent practice, and termination of services, among others. Authentic practitioner-client relationships, critics argue, depend on the kind of deep connection that only in-person contact enables. To provide effective behavioral health services, they claim, practitioners must be in the same room with clients to truly connect with them and ensure the degree of trust that is essential for effective helping. Services provided remotely greatly increase the likelihood that practitioners will miss important clinical cues—for example, tears welling up in a client's eyes, joyful facial expressions, or a client's grimace or squirm in response to the practitioner's probing question or comment. Further, practitioners who offer distance services may find it difficult to maintain clear boundaries in their relationships with clients, in part because of ambiguity surrounding the temporal limits of their interactions that are no longer limited to office-based visits during normal working hours. And, among other concerns, there are complex challenges related to protecting and managing client privacy and confidentiality.

CHAPTER TWO

The Contours of Online and Distance Behavioral Health

ETHICAL CHALLENGES

MENTAL HEALTH RESOURCES and services emerged on the Internet as early as 1982 in the form of online self-help support groups (Kanani & Regehr, 2003; Reamer, 2013a). The first known fee-based Internet mental health service was established by Sommers in 1995; by the late 1990s, groups of clinicians were forming companies and e-clinics that offered online counseling services to the public using secure websites (Skinner & Zack, 2004).

In behavioral health, the earliest discussions of electronic tools focused on practitioners' use of information technology (Schoech, 1999) and the ways in which practitioners could use Internet resources, such as online chat rooms and listservs joined by colleagues, professional networking sites, news groups, and email (Finn & Barak, 2010; Grant & Grobman, 1998; Martinez & Clark, 2000). Services now include a much wider range of digital and electronic options to serve clients who struggle with mental health and behavioral issues (Andersson, 2016; Chester & Glass, 2006; Glueckauf et al., 2018; Kanani & Regehr, 2003; Lamendola, 2010; Menon & Miller-Cribbs, 2002; Reamer, 2012a, 2013a, 2017; Rummell & Joyce, 2010; Zur, 2012).

ONLINE COUNSELING

Hundreds of online counseling services are now available to clients (Anderson & Guyton, 2013; Barak et al., 2008; Chang, 2005; McCarty & Clancy, 2002; Midkiff & Wyatt, 2008; Richards

& Vigano, 2013; Santhiveeran, 2009). People who struggle with depression, borderline and bipolar issues, addiction, marital and relationship conflict, anxiety, eating disorders, grief, and other mental health and behavioral challenges can use electronic search engines to locate practitioners who offer counseling services using live online chat (Haberstroh, 2009). Clients can purchase online therapeutic chat services in various time increments paid for by credit card. Live online chat is an example of what computer experts call synchronous communication (Mallen et al., 2011), meaning it occurs simultaneously in real time (Gupta & Agrawal, 2012). This contrasts with asynchronous communication, where communication is not synchronized or occurring simultaneously (for example, when a client sends a practitioner an email message regarding a clinical issue and waits for a time-delayed response).

TELEPHONE COUNSELING

Behavioral health professionals provide local and long-distance counseling services by telephone, sometimes to clients they never meet in person. After providing a counselor with a username and credit card information, clients receive telephone counseling. Some practitioners provide telephone counseling as a formal service. Others supplement traditional face-to-face counseling with occasional telephone counseling—for example, when clients or clinicians are traveling away from home or clients are in crisis situations.

VIDEO COUNSELING

Behavioral health professionals also offer clients live distance counseling using webcams, pan-tilt zoom cameras, and monitors. Some practitioners use video counseling software that claims to be HIPAA compliant, while others do not (Lindeman, 2011; Reamer, 2017).

CYBERTHERAPY AND AVATAR THERAPY

Some behavioral health professionals offer individual and group counseling services to clients using a 3-D virtual world where clients and practitioners interact with each other visually with avatars rather than real-life photos or live images. An avatar is a digitally generated graphic image, or caricature, that clients and practitioners use to represent themselves in a virtual world that appears on their computer screen.

Clients and practitioners join an online therapy community, create their avatars, and electronically enter a virtual therapy room for individual or group counseling.

SELF-GUIDED WEB-BASED INTERVENTIONS

Behavioral health professionals and their clients now have access to a wide variety of online interventions designed to help people who struggle with diverse mental health and behavioral issues. Users complete online questionnaires concerning their mental health and behavioral challenges, and then receive electronic or automated feedback and resources that can help them decide whether to address their issues. Users who indicate a wish for help are then provided links to service providers who offer distance counseling services.

SMARTPHONE APPS

Many behavioral health professionals incorporate smartphone apps as clinical tools that clients can use. An increasing number of clinical programs encourage or require clients to download apps on their smartphones to record information about their clinical symptoms, behaviors, and moods; receive automated messages from treatment providers, including positive and supportive messages; obtain psychoeducation information; and obtain links to local resources, including locations of 12-step meetings. Clients who want to avoid high-risk locations can program addresses into the app, which is programmed to send the client an electronic text warning if the client is in or near the high-risk location (for example, when a client who is in recovery wants to avoid certain high-risk neighborhoods).

Also, in some programs practitioners have the ability to enter information about clients into a smartphone app that can then be accessed remotely by colleagues who have subsequent encounters with the same client. For example, practitioners employed by a program that provides street outreach services to people who struggle with homelessness can summarize their encounters in the smartphone app immediately after the encounter, including information about the homeless individual's unique housing challenges, health and behavioral health concerns, and eligibility for public benefits and services. This shared digital access any time of the day or night helps to facilitate practitioners' coordination of services without relying on office-based records.

ELECTRONIC SOCIAL NETWORKS

Online social networking sites, such as Facebook, are now pervasive in both clients' and behavioral health professionals' lives (Lakhani, 2013). Some practitioners believe that maintaining online relationships with clients on social networking sites can be used as a therapeutic tool (Barak & Grohol, 2011; Graffeo & La Barbera, 2009; Lannin & Scott, 2013); they claim that informal contact with clients on social networking sites empowers clients, humanizes the relationship, and makes practitioners more accessible. Some practitioners—a small minority, it appears—are using social networking sites with clients much less formally. These clinicians believe that informal contact with clients on the practitioners' personal (not professional or agency-based) social networking site can be valuable therapeutically.

EMAIL

Many websites offer people the opportunity to receive mental health services by exchanging therapeutic email messages with behavioral health professionals. Typically, these practitioners invite users to email a therapy-related question for a flat fee and guarantee a response within 24–48 hours. Some practitioners offer clients monthly email packages that include a set number of email exchanges (e.g., six to eight). Other practitioners choose to exchange occasional clinically relevant emails with clients as an extension of their office-based services (Finn, 2006; Gutheil & Simon, 2005; Peterson & Beck, 2003; Zur, 2012).

TEXT MESSAGES

Some practitioners have chosen to exchange text messages with clients informally—for example, when clients wish to cancel or reschedule an appointment or provide the practitioner with a brief update during a crisis (Barak & Grohol, 2011; Reamer, 2017; Zur, 2012). Other practitioners and some social service programs have incorporated text messaging as a formal component in their intervention model. In these protocols, clinicians may draw on cognitive-behavioral treatment concepts to provide clients with automated positive and supportive text messages.

CASE EXAMPLES

Case A

A 42-year-old man, Darren G., felt desperate for mental health counseling. Earlier in the day, Mr. G. learned that the local police were planning to charge him with narcotics distribution. Mr. G. has struggled for years with symptoms of bipolar disorder. Over time, Mr. G. reports, he began to "self-medicate" with cocaine, developed an addiction, and began selling drugs to support his addiction. One night, at 11:15 p.m., Mr. G. was experiencing severe anxiety and felt he needed help, but knew he would not be able to find a therapist at that hour with whom he could meet in-person. Mr. G., who once was employed as a computer analyst and is comfortable with technology, went online and found a website that offers immediate online counseling from licensed clinicians. Mr. G. filled out a brief assessment form, provided his credit card information, and within five minutes connected online with a clinical psychologist who works more than 700 miles from Mr. G.'s home. The website did not include a detailed statement about encryption, confidentiality, anonymity, potential benefits and risks, and HIPAA compliance. The psychologist and Mr. G. had five online clinical encounters using live online chat and email. Over time Mr. G. became dissatisfied with the clinician's services. Eventually he filed a complaint with the psychologist's licensing board alleging that the clinician was not available consistently, did not respond to online messages, provided superficial assistance, and did not have a license to practice clinical psychology in Mr. G.'s state of residence, as required by law in Mr. G.'s state for distance counseling services.

Case B

A 52-year-old woman, Susanna C., telephoned an independent clinical social worker seeking counseling. Ms. C. explained that she recently divorced and was struggling as a single parent. Ms. C. reported that her child's father left the marriage suddenly and moved across the country to live with his new partner. She told the social worker that shortly after the divorce, she had received therapy briefly from a clinician at a community mental health center located about 48 miles from Ms. C.'s home in a very rural community. Ms. C. told the social worker whom she called—whose office was about 26 miles from Ms. C.s home—that she found the earlier counseling helpful but, due to living in a small town in a very remote part of the state and needing to be available to her young child, the driving distance posed a serious challenge.

Ms. C. asked the social worker if she could provide her with a combination of office-based and remote (online and video) counseling services; Ms. C. explained that traveling to the social worker's physical office weekly would be difficult, given the geographic distance and her parenting and work schedules, but, Ms. C. said, she understood the importance of occasional in-person meetings and was willing to make the drive sporadically if much of the counseling could be provided remotely. The social worker agreed to provide distance counseling services, including video sessions via Skype. The social worker was not aware that many health care attorneys do not consider basic Skype service to be HIPAA compliant.

Case C

A 29-year-old Marine Corps veteran, Amanda B., contacted the regional Veterans Administration center by telephone seeking counseling. Ms. B. had been diagnosed with post-traumatic stress disorder, generalized anxiety disorder, and opioid addiction following her medical discharge from the Marine Corps as a result of a serious injury she sustained during a training exercise. Ms. B. told the VA counselor she was eager to get counseling but had difficulty arranging transportation to the mental health clinic due to her anxiety and transportation challenges. She asked whether the VA would be able to provide her with remote video counseling. The VA offered Ms. B. synchronous (real time) distance counseling using its telehealth software. The mental health counselors who provided the distance counseling services received extensive training on the strengths and limitations of this therapeutic option and on ethical issues related to informed consent, privacy, confidentiality, privileged communication, provision of emergency services, documentation, and termination of services.

KEY ETHICAL ISSUES

Recent research and developments related to behavioral health practitioners' use of technology suggest that the most prominent ethical challenges concern several core, traditional ethics concepts pertaining to the delivery of services using digital technology: informed consent; privacy and confidentiality; boundaries, dual relationships, and conflicts of interest; practitioner competence; records and documentation; and collegial relationships (American Psychological Association, 2020; American Psychiatric Association, 2020; Association of Marital and Family Therapy Regulatory Boards, 2016; Association of Social Work Boards, 2015; Berg et al., 2001; Campbell & Gordon, 2003; Grimm et al., 2009; Hu et al., 2010; Mattison, 2012; Midkiff & Wyatt, 2008; Morgan

& Polowy, 2011; National Association of Social Workers [NASW], 2017; National Association of Social Workers et al., 2017; National Board for Certified Counselors, 2016a, 2016b; Reamer, 2013b, 2015; Recupero & Rainey, 2005; Recupero & Reamer, 2018; Sidell, 2015; Zur, 2007).

Informed Consent

Behavioral health professionals respect clients' right to consent to services (Berg et al., 2001; Reamer, 2013b, 2015). The advent of distance counseling and other remote social services delivered electronically has enhanced practitioners' ethical duty to ensure that clients fully understand the nature of these services and their potential benefits and risks. Obtaining clients' truly informed consent can be especially difficult when practitioners never meet clients in person or have the opportunity to speak with clients about informed consent. Special challenges arise when minors contact practitioners and request distance or remote services, particularly when practitioners offer services funded by contracts or grants and do not require payment from minor clients' parents or insurance companies; laws around the world vary considerably regarding minors' right to obtain services from behavioral health professionals without parental knowledge or consent (Reamer, 2015).

The concept of informed consent has always been prominent in behavioral health. Consistent with practitioners' longstanding embrace of the principle of client self-determination, informed consent procedures require practitioners to obtain clients' permission before releasing confidential information to third parties; allowing clients to be photographed, videotaped, or audiotaped by the media, professionals, or other parties; permitting clients to participate in treatment programs; or permitting clients to participate as subjects in research or evaluation projects. The concept of informed consent is now being extended to practitioners' delivery of online and distance services.

The historical roots of informed consent have been traced to Plato, who in *Laws* compares the coercive Greek slave-physician with the free physician who "takes the patient and his family into confidence ... [and] does not give prescriptions until he has won the patient's support." The medieval French surgeon Henri de Mondeville also stressed the importance of obtaining a patient's consent. By the late 18th century, European and American physicians and scientists had begun to develop a tradition that encouraged professionals to share information and decision-making with clients.

The first major legal ruling in the United States on informed consent was in the 1914 landmark case of *Schloendorff v. Society of New York Hospital*, in which Judge Benjamin Cardozo expressed his oft-cited opinion concerning an individual's right to self-determination: "Every human being of adult years and sound mind has a right to determine what shall be done with his own body." The phrase *informed consent* was introduced in the 1957 court case of *Salgo v. Leland Stanford Jr. University Board of Trustees*. The plaintiff in this case, who became paraplegic following a procedure for a circulatory problem, alleged that his physician did not properly disclose ahead of time essential information concerning risks.

State and federal laws and regulations vary in interpretations and applications of informed consent standards. In general, professionals agree that several conditions must be met for consent to be considered valid, and these longstanding standards are relevant to behavioral health professionals' provision of online and distance services:

1. *Coercion and undue influence must not have played a role in the client's decision.* Practitioners often maintain some degree of control over clients' lives (for example, by approving benefits, admission into programs, and the termination of services). Practitioners must ensure that clients do not feel pressured to grant consent to service provided remotely.

2. *A client must be mentally capable of providing consent.* Clearly, some clients (for example, young children and individuals who suffer from serious mental illness or dementia) are unable to comprehend the consent procedure. Other clients, however, may be only temporarily unable to consent, such as individuals who are under the influence of alcohol or other drugs at the time consent is sought or who experience transient psychotic symptoms. In general, practitioners should assess clients' ability to reason and make informed choices, comprehend relevant facts and retain this information, appreciate current circumstances, and communicate wishes. Clients who are unable to consent to online and distance services at a given moment may be able to consent in the future if the incapacity is temporary.

3. *Consent forms and procedures must be valid.* Practitioners sometimes present clients with general, broadly worded consent forms that may violate clients' right to be informed and may be considered invalid if challenged in a court of law. Practitioners should include details that refer to specific activities, information to be released, or interventions. Typical elements include details of the nature and purpose of a service or disclosure of information; advantages and disadvantages of an intervention; substantial or possible risks to clients, if any (including risks uniquely associated with online and distance behavioral health services); potential effects on clients' families, jobs, social activities, and other important aspects of their lives; alternatives to the proposed

intervention or disclosure; and anticipated costs for clients. All this information should be presented to clients in clear, understandable language and in a manner that encourages clients to ask questions for clarification. Consent forms should be dated and include a reasonable expiration date.

Practitioners should be especially sensitive to clients' cultural and ethnic differences related to the meaning of concepts such as "self-determination" and "consent." When necessary, forms should be translated into a client's primary language and competent interpreter services should be provided. Practitioners should never ask clients to sign blank consent forms, even when practitioners believe they have clients' permission to insert details at a later time. This arrangement cannot possibly constitute informed consent.

4. *A client must have the right to refuse or withdraw consent.* Practitioners should be prepared for the possibility that clients will exercise these rights, particularly with respect to the delivery of online and distance behavioral health services. Practitioners should inform clients of their rights and help clients make thoughtful and informed decisions based on all available facts and information about potential benefits and risks (Reamer, 2013b, 2015).

Practitioners' time-honored commitment to informed consent is based on the behavioral health professions' earnest embrace of clients' right to self-determination. The informed consent process is one of the clearest expressions of practitioners' respect for clients' rights (National Association of Social Workers et al., 2017). Such assessment can be especially challenging when practitioners interact with clients only electronically, do not meet with them in person, or have difficulty confirming their identity and age (Reamer, 2013b, 2015; Recupero & Rainey, 2005).

In Case A, for example, the psychologist must ensure that Mr. G. thoroughly understands the potential benefits and risks associated with distance counseling. According to the American Psychological Association's *Ethical Principles of Psychologists and Code of Conduct* (2017; standard 3.10[a]),

When psychologists conduct research or provide assessment, therapy, counseling, or consulting services in person or via electronic transmission or other forms of communication, they obtain the informed consent of the individual or individuals using language that is reasonably understandable to that person or persons except when conducting such activities without consent is mandated by law or governmental regulation or as otherwise provided in this Ethics Code.

Similarly, the Code of Ethics adopted by the American Association for Marriage and Family Therapy (2015) states:

> Prior to commencing therapy or supervision services through electronic means (including but not limited to phone and Internet), marriage and family therapists ensure that they are compliant with all relevant laws for the delivery of such services. Additionally, marriage and family therapists must: (a) determine that technologically-assisted services or supervision are appropriate for clients or supervisees, considering professional, intellectual, emotional, and physical needs; (b) inform clients or supervisees of the potential risks and benefits associated with technologically-assisted services; (c) ensure the security of their communication medium; and (d) only commence electronic therapy or supervision after appropriate education, training, or supervised experience using the relevant technology. (standard 6.1)

When behavioral health professionals provide services to clients remotely, the informed consent form should include statements that address:

- The nature of the services that the practitioner will provide remotely, such as video counseling, text-based counseling, and smartphone applications.

- Possible benefits of remote service delivery. This may include geographical and scheduling convenience.

- Differences between services provided face-to-face and remotely.

- The skills and equipment (such as computer specifications and smartphone applications) the client will need to receive services remotely.

- The importance of privacy for both practitioner and client. Describe steps clients can take to ensure privacy. Describe steps you will take to ensure privacy (for example, use of encryption, firewalls, and data back-up software).

- The possibility of technology failure and transmission interruption, along with instructions in the event these occur (for example, call-back protocols).

- The possibility that stored data could be accessed by unauthorized people or companies, and the steps you will take to prevent this.

- An emergency response plan to address crises that may arise. Details may include names and telephone numbers of individuals the practitioner can contact, telephone numbers the client can call, and when the client should access care at the client's local hospital emergency department.

- Steps you will take if you believe that the client needs to access face-to-face services because of their clinical needs. Include details about referral and termination-of-service protocols.

- Guidelines for clients' use of email and text messaging to communicate with the practitioner (that is, whether electronic communications should be used only for administrative and scheduling purposes, as opposed to counseling issues).

- Agreement that the client will not record any remote counseling sessions or other discussions, unless agreed upon in advance.

Privacy and Confidentiality

Behavioral health professionals have always understood their obligation to protect client privacy and confidentiality and to be familiar with widely recognized exceptions (for example, when mandatory reporting laws concerning abuse and neglect require disclosure of information without client consent, or when laws or court orders require disclosure without client consent during legal proceedings). The concept of privacy in professional practice to a great extent is rooted in pronouncements by the Pythagoreans in the 4th century B.C.E. and was later incorporated in the Hippocratic oath: "Whatever I see or hear, in the life of men, which ought not to be spoken of abroad, I will not divulge, as reckoning that all such should be kept secret." The concept of privacy was also an important component of ancient Jewish law, as conveyed in the Talmud. Early English common law also acknowledged the right to privacy associated with the concept of honor among gentlemen (Reamer, 2015).

The new American states legally codified privacy rights in 1791 in the Fourth and Fifth Amendments to the U.S. Constitution. However, medical privacy had no legal basis until 1828, when the State of New York established the physician-patient privilege.

The rapid emergence of digital technology and other electronic media used by behavioral health professionals to deliver services has added a new layer of challenging privacy and confidentiality issues. Fortunately, sophisticated encryption technology can protect client confidentiality very effectively, although it is not foolproof; many professionals believe that encryption offers significantly more protection than do traditional paper documents (Hu et al., 2010).

Practitioners who offer video counseling services must recognize that they have much less control over confidentiality than when they provide traditional office-based services. For example, a client receiving video counseling services may invite a family member or acquaintance to sit in on a session—outside of camera range—without the practitioner's knowledge or consent.

Encryption of behavioral health services provided online is more challenging with some forms of technology than others. With regard to Skype, for example, National Association of Social Workers attorneys reviewed relevant research and legal guidelines and concluded that "assuring that clients' confidential communications via Skype will be adequately protected is a difficult and uncertain task" (Morgan & Polowy, 2011, p. 1). Practitioners cannot assume that Internet sites and electronic tools they use are necessarily encrypted. For example, the social worker in Case B, who may use email, live chat, and video counseling in her work with Ms. C.—both formally and informally—must be sure to use sophisticated encryption technology to prevent confidentiality breaches (hacking) by unauthorized parties and to comply with strict HIPAA guidelines, unless federal or state law permits exceptions (for example, during a national emergency).

The mental health counselor serving Ms. C. must also recognize that email communications for therapeutic purposes create a permanent record of online messages (known as a digital footprint); this would not occur in a typical in-office clinical session. Also, the counselor may have no control over what email messages Ms. C. chooses to share with other parties, in the form of forwarded or copied messages.

These novel confidentiality issues are addressed directly in several codes of ethics in the behavioral health professions. For example, according to the NASW Code of Ethics (2017): "Social workers should take reasonable steps to protect the confidentiality of electronic communications, including information provided to clients or third parties. Social workers should use applicable safeguards (such as encryption, firewalls, and passwords) when using electronic communications such as email, online posts, online chat sessions, mobile communication, and text messages" (standard 1.07[m]). Further, the NASW et al. (2017) technology standards state, "When using technology to deliver services, social workers shall establish and maintain confidentiality policies and procedures consistent with relevant statutes, regulations, rules, and ethical standards" (standard 2.07). The National Board for Certified Counselors Code of Ethics (2016a) states that practitioners "... shall act in a professional manner by protecting against unauthorized access to confidential information. This includes data contained in electronic formats. ..." (standard 56). Practitioners are wise not to assume that Internet sites and electronic tools they use are necessarily encrypted; the ethical burden is on the practitioner to ensure trustworthy encryption by carefully examining statements and guarantees made by software vendors.

To practice ethically, behavioral health professionals who use digital and other technology to provide distance services must develop privacy and confidentiality protocols that include several key elements. Practitioners must review and adhere to relevant laws and regulations, including federal laws (for example, 42 CFR Part 2 and HIPAA) and state laws pertaining to the confidentiality of health and mental health records and exceptions to clients' right to confidentiality to protect clients and third parties from harm.

Further, practitioners must use sound judgment about conducting online searches to gather information about clients (using widely used online search engines) without clients' knowledge or consent; some clients may feel over exposed and violated by clinicians' attempts to conduct online searches for information about them (Clinton et al., 2010). According to the NASW Code of Ethics (2017), "social workers should avoid searching or gathering client information electronically unless there are compelling professional reasons, and when appropriate, with the client's informed consent" (standard 1.07[q]).

Thus, the presumption is that practitioners will generally respect client privacy and avoid searching online for information about clients without their knowledge or consent. As the NASW Code of Ethics states, however, there are exceptional instances when it may be ethical for social workers to conduct such online searches for information about clients. Examples might include situations where a high-risk, vulnerable client has disappeared and not been in contact with the social worker, or when a social worker who provides home-based services searches publicly available judicial databases to determine whether there may be a safety risk during home visits. Consistent with these guidelines, behavioral health professionals and their employers would do well to establish written policies and protocols that spell out when such online searches are appropriate and the criteria and procedures practitioners should use to make these determinations.

Also, behavioral health professionals must develop confidentiality agreements when conducting group treatment or facilitating support groups online. As with in-person group sessions, practitioners should ensure that clients adhere to appropriate confidentiality guidelines and agree to respect other group members' privacy.

In addition, practitioners must know how to respond to subpoenas and court orders to release what lawyers refer to as electronically stored information (ESI); legal and ethical standards are evolving regarding third parties' right to ESI during legal proceedings and clinicians' ability to protect this information (Grimm et al., 2009). In Case A, for example, a prosecutor subpoenaed Mr. G.'s psychologist's electronic records, including email and text message exchanges between Mr. G. and the practitioner, in conjunction with the criminal investigation. The prosecutor sought evidence of any disclosures Mr. G. might have made to his psychologist concerning his alleged criminal activity.

During their graduate school years, most contemporary behavioral health professionals did not learn about how to protect ESI; until recently, this content was not included in behavioral health education curricula. ESI is generally defined as all information stored in computers and other electronic or digital devices. This includes email, voicemail, instant and text messages, databases, metadata, and any other digital images and files. During legal proceedings (such as when practitioners' clients are involved in termination of parental rights proceedings, child custody disputes, divorce proceedings, malpractice litigation, workers compensation proceedings, and criminal court matters), attorneys may seek to access practitioners' ESI, usually through subpoenas and court orders. In fact, there is now a subspecialty known in legal circles as e-discovery, which refers to any process in which electronic data are sought, located, secured, and searched with the intent of using it as evidence in a civil or criminal legal case.

Attorneys now learn how to access ESI and about pertinent legal guidelines concerning what can and cannot be discovered. For example, the Federal Rules of Civil Procedure, which, since 1938, have governed court procedure for civil cases in federal courts, have been amended to include guidelines pertaining to discovery of ESI. The rules now state that a party in a civil matter may formally request that another party "produce and permit the requesting party or its representative to inspect, copy, test, or sample the following items in the responding party's possession, custody, or control ... any designated documents or electronically stored information—including writings, drawings, graphs, charts, photographs, sound recordings, images, and other data or data compilations—stored in any medium from which information can be obtained either directly or, if necessary, after translation by the responding party into a reasonably usable form" (Rule 34).

The emergence of ESI is yet another example of how contemporary behavioral health professionals need to think very differently about how they function in the digital age, especially with respect to their compliance with ethical standards. To protect clients (and themselves), practitioners should apply time-honored ethical standards when managing ESI, especially related to client privacy, confidentiality, informed consent, documentation, boundaries, and management of records. Practitioners should be especially mindful of emerging ethical standards pertaining to protection and encryption of clients' sensitive information, disclosures of ESI in response to subpoenas and court orders, retention and destruction of electronic records, and clients' right to access their electronic records through online portals. These phenomena require practitioners to think outside the box and to appreciate the relatively new fact that each time they record or share information electronically, they automatically—and possibly irrevocably—create permanent records and digital trails that require unprecedented ethical judgment.

Also, behavioral health professionals should ensure that their means of electronic data gathering adhere to the privacy and security standards of applicable laws. These laws may address electronic transactions, client rights, and allowable disclosure (Association of Social Work Boards, 2015). Increasing numbers of behavioral health programs and individual practitioners are conducting what are known as privacy audits to ensure compliance with current standards. Many of the current privacy audit standards were developed with two prominent sets of federal standards—HIPAA and the Health Information Technology for Economic and Clinical Health (HITECH) Act—in mind. HIPAA, which has become the gold standard related to privacy, is very well known. As most behavioral health professionals know, the Health Insurance Portability and Accountability Act (Public Law 104–191, 110 Stat. 1936) was enacted in 1996 by the U.S. Congress and signed by President Bill Clinton. HIPAA sets the standard for protecting sensitive client data. Any health care provider that deals with protected health information (PHI) must ensure that all of the required physical, network, and process security measures are in place and followed.

Less well known is the HITECH Act, part of the American Recovery and Reinvestment Act of 2009, which includes provisions requiring organizations to conduct privacy audits. Subtitle D of the HITECH Act addresses the privacy and security concerns associated with the electronic transmission of health information, in part through several provisions that strengthen the civil and criminal enforcement of the HIPAA rules. Health care organizations and third-party payers are expected to monitor for breaches of PHI from both internal and external sources.

In 2012, the U.S. Office for Civil Rights released criteria that its auditors use to validate compliance with federal regulations. They provide a useful guide for organizations that offer behavioral health services and that conduct their own privacy audits. Key audit activities include the following:

- Determine the activities that will be tracked or audited. Obtain and review documentation to determine whether audit controls have been implemented over information systems that contain or use PHI.

- Select the tools that will be deployed for auditing and system activity reviews. Inquire of management as to whether systems and applications have been evaluated to determine whether upgrades are necessary. Obtain and review documentation of tools or applications that management has identified to capture the appropriate audit information.

- Develop and deploy the information review/audit policy. Obtain and review formal or informal policies and procedures and evaluate the content to understand whether a formal audit policy is in place to communicate the details of the entity's audits and reviews to the workforce. Obtain and review an email, or some form of communication, showing that the audit policy is communicated to the workforce.

- Develop appropriate standard operating procedures. Obtain and review management's procedures in place to determine the systems and applications to be audited and how they will be audited.

The American Health Information Management Association (AHIMA)—a prominent organization dedicated to improving the management of health-related information—has developed comprehensive protocols for professionals who want to conduct privacy audits. Their guidelines are especially valuable for behavioral health professionals and agencies. According to AHIMA, privacy audits should produce detailed audit logs that are useful for the following:

- detecting unauthorized access to client information;
- establishing a culture of responsibility and accountability;
- reducing the risk associated with inappropriate access;
- providing forensic evidence during investigations of suspected and known security incidents and breaches to client privacy, especially if sanctions against a workforce member, business associate, or other contracted agent will be applied;
- tracking disclosures of PHI;
- responding to client privacy concerns regarding unauthorized access by family members, friends, or others;
- evaluating the overall effectiveness of the organization's policy and user education regarding appropriate access and use of client information (this includes comparing actual workforce activity to expected activity and discovering where additional training or education may be necessary to reduce errors);
- detecting new threats and intrusion attempts;
- identifying potential problems; and
- addressing compliance with regulatory and accreditation requirements.

Unfortunately, a number of behavioral health professionals and their employers have discovered significant security breaches that led to online exposure of clients' sensitive health and behavioral health information. For example, Sunshine Behavioral Health Group, a network of drug and alcohol addiction treatment facilities in California, Colorado, and Texas, experienced a breach of sensitive patient information due to a misconfigured website. News reports indicate that breached data included billing records that may have contained some combination of full names, birth dates, addresses, telephone numbers, email addresses, credit card numbers, expiration dates, CVV (card verification value) codes, and health insurance information (Alden, 2020).

In another case, Inmediata Health Group, a provider of clearing-house services, software, and business processing solutions to health plans, hospitals, and independent practitioners, disclosed a security incident affecting some customer data. The incident was discovered when Inmediata found that a misconfigured webpage was allowing some electronic health information to be viewed publicly. The webpage was allowing search engines to index Inmediata's internal webpages that were used for business operations and not intended for public view. The health information involved in this incident included patients' names, dates of birth, genders, and medical claims information, with some affected individuals potentially having their Social Security numbers exposed (Gross, 2019).

In addition, personal data of more than 645,000 clients of Oregon's Department of Human Services were compromised during a data breach. The breached client information potentially included first and last names, addresses, dates of birth, Social Security numbers, case numbers, personal health information, and other information used in DHS programs. The data breach occurred as a result of an email phishing attempt when several DHS employees opened and clicked on a phishing link, thereby giving the sender access to their accounts (Chaffin, 2019).

In one widely publicized case, the U.S. Federal Trade Commission (FTC) charged an electronic health records company with deceptive practices that violated patients' privacy and confidentiality (Federal Trade Commission, 2016). The cloud-based electronic health record company agreed to settle FTC charges that it misled consumers by soliciting reviews for their doctors without disclosing adequately that these reviews would be publicly posted on the Internet, resulting in the public disclosure of patients' sensitive personal and medical information.

According to the FTC complaint, the company made plans to launch a public-facing healthcare provider directory. In order to populate the directory with patient reviews, the company began sending email messages to patients of healthcare providers utilizing the company's electronic health records service. The emails appeared to be sent on behalf of the patients' doctors and asked consumers to rate their provider "[t]o help improve your service in the future."

According to the complaint, consumers who clicked on the five-star rating image in the email were taken to an online survey form with questions about their recent medical visit. The survey included a text box where patients could enter any information they wished within a set character limit. Because patients likely thought the information was only shared with their provider, many of them included in the text box their full name or phone number along with personal health information inquiries. For instance,

- one consumer asked for information on dosing for "my Xanax prescription";

- one consumer included a request for help with a depressed child, writing "I think she is depressed and has stated several times this week that she wishes she was dead"; and

- one consumer wrote that "I did a little research and I think I have a yeast infection called candida."

The settlement with the FTC prohibited the company from making deceptive statements about the privacy or confidentiality of the information it collects from consumers. It also required the company, prior to making any consumers' information publicly available, to clearly and conspicuously disclose this fact and obtain consumers' affirmative consent.

Boundaries, Dual Relationships, and Conflicts of Interest

Throughout the history of the behavioral health professions, practitioners have understood their duty to avoid conflicts of interest that may harm clients (Brownlee, 1996; Campbell & Gordon, 2003; Daley & Doughty, 2006; Reamer, 2012b, 2018c; Zur, 2007). Practitioners' use of digital technology has introduced new and complicated boundary issues. Many practitioners receive requests from current and former clients asking to be social networking "friends" or contacts (Kolmes & Taube, 2016). Electronic contact with clients and former clients on social networking sites can lead to boundary confusion (Gabbard, Kassaw, & Perez-Garcia, 2011; MacDonald, Sohn, & Ellis, 2010). Electronic message exchanges between practitioners and clients that occur outside of normal business hours, especially if the practitioner uses a personal social networking site or email address, may confuse practitioner–client boundaries. Practitioners who choose not to accept a client's "friend" request on a social networking site to maintain clear boundaries may inadvertently cause the client to feel a deep sense of rejection. Practitioners should anticipate this possibility and explain to clients how they handle clients' Facebook requests.

In one licensing board case in which I testified as an expert witness, a counselor was disciplined after a complaint was filed against him by the father of the practitioner's minor client. According to the licensing board's findings, the counselor exchanged a large number of very personal Facebook and text messages with his client, often late at night. In some of the messages, the counselor asked the client about her sexual experiences. Several of the messages included information that the counselor disclosed to the client about the counselor's personal struggles and disappointments. The licensing board revoked the counselor's license after he failed to comply with conditions imposed by the board.

Also, clients who are able to access practitioners' publicly available social networking sites may learn a great deal of personal information about their practitioner (such as information about the practitioner's personal and family relationships, social and religious activities, and political views); this may introduce complex boundary challenges in the practitioner-client relationship (Kolmes & Taube, 2016). Some practitioners have managed this risk by creating two distinct Facebook sites, one for professional use (known as a Facebook page) and one for personal use (Facebook profile).

Also, clients' postings on their own social networking sites may lead to inadvertent or harmful disclosure of private and confidential details—for example, sensitive information shared by others in group therapy sessions.

Behavioral health professionals who do not maintain strict privacy settings on their online social networking sites expose themselves to considerable risk. In one highly publicized case, a social worker was disciplined by her regulatory board in response to a complaint filed by a client who discovered that the social worker posted publicly available comments about the client on the social worker's personal Facebook site. At the time, the client had a Child Protective Services case pending in court. The social worker posted on Facebook: "I'm in court tomorrow for a case where there is a high level of domestic violence amongst many things ..." and after the trial concluded posted: "It's powerful to know that ... children's lives have just massively changed for the better and now they are safe and protected from harm and have every hope for the future ..." One of the social worker's online posts was accompanied by a small map, pinpointing the location of the court.

The social worker's defense during the board hearing was that "she had believed that her Facebook page was accessible only to her 'friends,' not the wider public as a result of her privacy settings." However, the post was publicly available and was found by her manager through a Google search of her name (Stevenson, 2014).

Further, newer forms of distance counseling may introduce conflicts of interest that were previously unknown in behavioral health. For example, some video counseling sites are offered free to practitioners; the websites' sponsors pay for their development and maintenance. In return, sponsors post electronic links on the counseling screen that take users to their websites that include information about their products and services. Clients may believe that their practitioners endorse these products and services or benefit from sales.

To practice ethically, practitioners who use digital and other technology to provide distance services must develop protocols concerning boundaries, dual relationships, and conflicts of interest that include several key elements. Practitioners must develop sound guidelines governing their contact with current and former clients on social networking sites (for example, Facebook, LinkedIn) and their willingness to provide services to people they first met socially on social networking sites. Practitioners must be careful to avoid inappropriate disclosure of personal information in digital communications (for example, email messages, text messages, and social network postings) and should establish clear guidelines concerning interactions with clients online and via other digital and electronic means at various times of day and night, weekends, and holidays.

The 24/7/365 access that digital communications make possible creates elastic boundaries that are new to behavioral health professionals who otherwise have been able to maintain clear boundaries when services are provided in person during traditional working hours (Greysen et al., 2012). Practitioners must also think carefully about maintaining digital and electronic relationships with former clients; easy access via electronic means can introduce ethical and clinical challenges related to boundaries and dependency. For example, the NASW Code of Ethics includes several relevant standards:

> Social workers should avoid communication with clients using technology (such as social networking sites, online chat, e-mail, text messages, telephone, and video) for personal or non-work-related purposes. (standard 1.06[e])
>
> Social workers should be aware that posting personal information on professional Web sites or other media might cause boundary confusion, inappropriate dual relationships, or harm to clients. (standard 1.06[f])
>
> Social workers should be aware that personal affiliations may increase the likelihood that clients may discover the social worker's presence on Web sites, social media, and other forms of technology. Social workers should be aware that involvement in electronic communication with groups based on race, ethnicity, language, sexual orientation, gender identity or expression, mental or physical ability, religion, immigration status, and other personal affiliations may affect their ability to work effectively with particular clients. (standard 1.06[g])

Social workers should avoid accepting requests from or engaging in personal relationships with clients on social networking sites or other electronic media to prevent boundary confusion, inappropriate dual relationships, or harm to clients. (standard 1.06[h])

Practitioner Competence

Behavioral health professionals have always recognized the importance of competent practice, whether they are in clinical, supervisory, or managerial roles. The emergence of digital tools and other technology-driven options has added a new set of essential competencies for practitioners who choose to incorporate them in their work. Use of this technology requires a great deal of technical mastery in addition to awareness of, and compliance with, rapidly developing standards of care and ethical guidelines.

To practice ethically, practitioners who use digital and other technology to provide distance services—such as the psychologist in Case A who used online chat to provide crisis services to Mr. G. and the social worker in Case B who used videoconferencing to counsel Ms. C.—must seek training and continuing education focused explicitly on the use of distance counseling technology, including developing protocols for screening potential clients, obtaining clients' informed consent, assessing clients' clinical needs, maintaining confidentiality, implementing distance interventions and services, maintaining clear boundaries, managing documentation and client records, and terminating services (Reamer, 2019). According to the Association of Marital and Family Therapy Regulatory Boards (2016) teletherapy guidelines, therapists must "demonstrate continued competence in a variety of ways (e.g., encryption of data, HIPAA compliant connections)." Areas to be covered in the training include appropriateness of teletherapy; teletherapy theory and practice; modes of delivery; legal and ethical issues; handling online emergencies; best practices; and informed consent, among other topics.

According to national standards promulgated by the National Association of Social Workers et al. (2017), "social workers who use technology to provide services shall obtain and maintain the knowledge and skills required to do so in a safe, competent, and ethical manner" (standard 2.06). Such knowledge and skills include knowing how to communicate effectively while using the technology to provide services; handle emergency situations from a remote location; apply the laws of both the practitioner's and client's location; be sensitive to the client's culture, including the client's cultural community and linguistic, social, and economic environment; attend to clients' unique needs and challenges; ensure that the technology is in working order to provide effective services and avoid disruption; keep abreast of the changing landscape of technology; and adapt accordingly.

Behavioral health professionals, such as the psychologist in Case A who provided Mr. G. with counseling services that were delivered electronically across state lines, must keep current with evolving licensing laws and regulations regarding provision of distance counseling services across jurisdictional lines. Many states' laws prohibit practitioners from providing distance services that are received in states in which the practitioners do not hold a license, unless there are emergency circumstances recognized by law (Telehealth Resource Center, 2020).

Records and Documentation

Maintaining high-quality records is essential in behavioral health, especially when practitioners provide clinical and casework services. Records are necessary for thorough client assessment; planning and delivering services; being accountable to clients, insurers, agencies, other providers, courts, and utilization review organizations; ensuring continuity and coordination of services; providing quality supervision; and evaluating services (Sidell, 2015). Practitioners' use of online and other electronic services poses significant documentation challenges. Behavioral health professionals must develop strict protocols to ensure that professionally relevant email, text, and social networking (for example, Facebook) exchanges are documented properly in case records. These are relatively new expectations that are not reflected in the behavioral health professions' longstanding training and literature on documentation (Sidell, 2015). Practitioners must develop documentation procedures that meet professional standards of care and comply with laws and regulations concerning the protection of electronically stored information.

For example, the private-sector clinicians who plan to serve Mr. G. (Case A) and Ms. C. (Case B) must develop documentation procedures that meet professional standards of care and comply with federal (for example, HIPAA) and state regulations concerning the protection of electronically stored clinical information. Practitioners employed in public-sector settings, such as the mental health counselor in Case C, must ensure that their employers have documentation protocols that meet the profession's ethical standards.

To practice ethically, practitioners who use digital and other technology to provide distance services must develop records and documentation protocols that include several key elements. Practitioners must develop guidelines that ensure proper encryption; reasonable and appropriate access by clients and colleagues to electronic records and documents (for example, when a practitioner is incapacitated and a colleague provides coverage); documentation of video counseling sessions, email, text messages, and cybertherapy communications; compliance with laws, regulations, and agency policies concerning record and document retention; and proper disposal and destruction of documents and records.

Many insurance companies now cover remote counseling and require practitioners to comply with strict documentation guidelines to protect client privacy and confidentiality. Many behavioral health professionals subscribe to HIPAA-compliant online software packages to ensure proper protection.

Practitioners who maintain electronic records should be familiar with HIPAA's specific protection of what this law refers to as "psychotherapy notes." The federal law, known as the Privacy Rule, defines psychotherapy notes as notes recorded by a health care provider who is a mental health professional documenting or analyzing the contents of a conversation during a private, group, joint, or family counseling session and that are *separate* from the rest of the client's health record (for example, a separate tab in the electronic record labeled "psychotherapy notes"). Psychotherapy notes, also called process or private notes, are notes taken by a mental health professional during a session with a client. Psychotherapy notes usually include the practitioner's impressions regarding diagnosis, observations, and any thoughts or feelings they have about a client's unique situation. After clinical encounters, practitioners can refer to their notes when determining an effective treatment plan.

To be considered "psychotherapy notes" under the law, these notes must be kept separate from clients' general records and billing information, and practitioners are not permitted to share psychotherapy notes with third parties without a client's authorization; even the client does not have the right to access these notes. In general, psychotherapy notes might include clinical observations, hypotheses, questions to ask supervisors, and any thoughts or feelings relating to the counseling session. Unlike traditional progress notes, psychotherapy notes are private and do not include medication details or records, test results, summaries of diagnosis or treatment plans, summaries of symptoms and prognosis, and summaries of client progress.

Psychotherapy notes receive special protection under the federal Privacy Rule because they contain sensitive information and because they are a therapist's personal notes. They do not contain information related to a client's health records, treatment, or healthcare operations, and therefore do not need to be shared with clients or staff. Psychotherapy notes provide behavioral health professionals with a memory jog, as needed.

Electronic Records

Practitioners who enter progress notes, psychotherapy notes, and other important information in electronic records should be aware of possible risks. In addition to the possibility (not necessarily the probability) of security breaches, behavioral health professionals must avoid what has become known as "copy and paste bloat," which occurs when, to save time, practitioners copy previous entries into a new note (Siegler & Adelman, 2009; Sulmasy et al., 2017). Hasty copying and pasting, especially without careful proofreading, can lead to significant errors. The "pasted" note may include details that are not accurate and that can lead to misinterpretation when reviewed by agency colleagues. In addition to perpetuating inaccuracies, such copying and pasting can constitute fraud. There is also the related risk of "note bloat" in electronic records. This occurs when copied and pasted notes include excessive extraneous details (Sulmasy et al., 2017).

Another risk associated with electronic records is the problem of "auto-population." Some practitioners' and behavioral health agencies' electronic records automatically populate, or fill in, different data fields when a user logs into a record. This can lead to inaccuracies when the data that are filled in automatically are not current (Sukel, 2019). Careful proofreading is essential. In one court case in which I served as an expert witness, a large social service agency was sued by surviving family members of a toddler who died. The toddler had been placed in foster care soon after her birth because of her mother's significant substance use and mental health challenges. The court ordered the infant's mother to receive behavioral health services from the agency.

A behavioral health practitioner who conducted a comprehensive assessment at the beginning of the service delivery period wrote a note in the electronic record summarizing his concerns about whether the mother would be able to parent the child. This note reappeared each time an agency staffer opened the electronic record and the software automatically updated the date of the note to reflect the date the record was opened. No one on the staff caught the formatting error that repeatedly changed the date of the note.

The agency staffers provided the mother with comprehensive services for more than one year, including mental health counseling, substance use disorder counseling, and parenting skills training. The mother was generally compliant with services and, the records indicated, made significant progress. The agency ultimately recommended to the court that the child be placed with the mother, along with continued supportive services. The court authorized the placement.

The child died about four months after she was placed with the mother; the mother was charged with murder. Surviving family members sued the agency, alleging that the agency was negligent when it recommended placement of the child with the mother. During the civil suit trial, at which I testified, the plaintiffs' attorneys highlighted the fact that the agency's electronic record included a note, dated the week when the staffers recommended that the child be placed with the mother, summarizing the staffer's concerns about the mother's ability to parent. In fact, that note had been written more than a year earlier, but the entry date was continually updated because of the electronic record's auto-population feature. At trial, neither I nor any other witness was able to prove that the inaccurately dated note had been written more than a year before the agency recommended placement of the child with the mother. The jury returned a multi-million-dollar verdict against the agency.

Behavioral health professionals who use electronic records must also be sure to log off once they have completed their entries. If they fail to log off, another staffer's subsequent entries could be mistakenly attributed to the practitioner who neglected to log off. This, too, could expose the practitioner who did not log off to significant malpractice risk if the notes that are wrongly attributed to the practitioner contain errors or are substandard.

Many behavioral health professionals can now access clients' electronic records remotely. This is convenient, of course, especially when a practitioner is on-call after hours and needs to access up-to-date client information during a consultation. However, this remote access also comes with risks. For example, practitioners who access clients' records from their homes must ensure that family members do not access the online information inappropriately (for example, if a family member uses the practitioner's computer). Behavioral health professionals must be vigilant in their efforts to protect client privacy.

In one case, a dedicated counselor employed by a prominent mental health center was housebound because of a blizzard. The agency director asked professional staffers, all of whom were able to access their encrypted clinical records from home by logging into the agency's database, to do as much work from home as possible. The counselor used this opportunity to bring his clinical notes up to date. He logged in to the records of clients he had seen the day before and completed his notes. The counselor took a selfie as he worked from home, sitting at his computer, and posted the photo on his Facebook page with the following caption: "We're completely snowed in today, but I'm so dedicated I'm working from home. See?!"

What the counselor failed to realize was that the photo he posted included considerable identifying information from his client's electronic record that was on the counselor's computer screen when he took the photo. The counselor's supervisor, who was the counselor's Facebook friend, saw the photo, enlarged the image on her computer screen, and was able to read detailed identifying information (PHI, according to HIPAA), including the client's clinical diagnoses. Clearly, this violated the client's privacy and, as well, strict federal and state confidentiality laws.

Another potential risk is associated with what have become known as client portals. An increasing number of behavioral health programs, especially those linked to hospitals and other integrated care settings, permit clients to access all or a portion of their electronic records by logging in with a unique username and password. On the one hand, allowing clients to access their records can enhance their knowledge about their condition and active involvement in their care. On the other hand, this access can lead to privacy breaches and client misunderstanding of the electronic record's content (for example, misinterpreting the language in a behavior health practitioner's clinical diagnoses and narratives). To reduce risk, practitioners and agencies that permit clients to access their electronic record should develop guidelines that include a number of key elements:

To protect client privacy and prevent security breaches:

- Require each client to register with a unique username and password.
- Carefully screen any sensitive client information that might be posted.
- Discuss portal access guidelines in all privacy and security policies and procedures that are provided to clients.
- Discuss policies related to clients' use of portals in your annual information technology security risk assessment.

To reduce the risk of inappropriate client use of portals:

- Describe appropriate and inappropriate use.
- Describe how clients may communicate through the portal and what they should expect for a response turnaround time.
- Describe the extent to which clients are permitted to upload information to their electronic record, including the content of information that is acceptable.
- Have the client sign a portal user agreement. Provide the client with a signed copy of the agreement.
- Include information on the portal entry page about guidelines for use, including that it should not be used for emergencies. Include instructions in the event of an emergency.
- Follow relevant federal and state laws related to privacy, confidentiality, privileged communication, and informed consent. Legal consultation may be appropriate.

- Create policies governing use of the portal by minors, including access to information in the portal by minors' parents and guardians.

To protect clients and reduce risk, behavioral health professionals who use electronic records should develop guidelines and protocols that include these key elements:

- Avoid cutting and pasting.
- Understand the software's automatic populating features and their implications. Where appropriate, delete the automatic population function.
- Periodically print out a representative sample of client records and review them for accuracy and clarity.
- Understand the ways in which the software creates a digital footprint and permanent record of each key stroke and entry. Identify which parties may be able to access the electronic record and potential implications for clients and service providers.
- Create security protections on hardware (including portable devices) and software. In addition to encryption, the software should include an automatic lock-out after a specified period of inactivity.
- Ensure compliance with federal and state confidentiality laws. Enter into appropriate confidentiality agreements with third parties that may access clients' electronic health records.

Collegial Relationships

Behavioral health professionals have long understood their ethical duty to treat colleagues with respect. Traditionally, collegial interactions among practitioners have occurred in person, in the context of agency-based meetings, and by telephone. Increasingly, however, collegial interactions are occurring online and in other remote forms, thus requiring new protocols and guidelines governing these interactions. This issue is addressed in the NASW et al. (2017) practice standards related to technology: "Social workers who communicate using electronic tools shall treat colleagues with respect and shall represent accurately and fairly the qualifications, views, and obligations of colleagues" (standard 3.11).

More specifically, in their relationships with colleagues involving technology, practitioners should abide by professional values and ethical standards when communicating with and about colleagues, avoiding cyberbullying, online harassment, or making derogatory or defamatory comments; avoid disclosing private, confidential, or sensitive information about the work or personal life of any colleague without consent, including messages, photographs, videos, or any other material that could invade or compromise a colleague's privacy; take reasonable steps to correct or remove any inaccurate or offensive information they have posted online or transmitted about a colleague using technology; acknowledge the work of and contributions made by others and avoid using technology to present the work of others as their own; take appropriate action if they believe that a colleague who provides electronic services is behaving unethically, is not using appropriate safeguards, or is allowing unauthorized access to electronically stored information; and use professional judgment and take steps to discourage, prevent, expose, and correct any efforts by colleagues who knowingly produce, possess, download, or transmit illicit or illegal content or images in electronic format. Such action may include discussing their concerns with the colleague when feasible and when such discussion is likely to produce a resolution; if there is no resolution, practitioners should report through appropriate formal channels established by employers, professional organizations, and governmental regulatory bodies (see NASW Code of Ethics, section 2.10).

In one case, I received a telephone call from an administrator of a state licensing board. She explained that the board had received a complaint filed by one practitioner against another. The administrator explained that the complainant and respondent worked at the same mental health center. The complainant was the respondent's supervisor. The respondent became quite angry with her supervisor after the supervisor included some negative comments in the respondent's annual review.

According to the complaint filed by the supervisor, the respondent posted a series of derogatory comments about the supervisor on the respondent's Facebook site. The respondent accused the supervisor publicly of being incompetent and unethical. The respondent did not realize that her supervisor had access to her Facebook posts, which the supervisor printed out and shared with the licensing board. The board issued a formal reprimand of the respondent, which is featured on the board's publicly available website.

In addition to violating ethical standards, practitioners who make derogatory comments about colleagues using online and digital technology expose themselves to legal risks in the form of a defamation of character lawsuit. For example, in the licensing board case about which I was consulted, the administrator told me that the complainant had also filed a lawsuit against the respondent. This moved the ethics-related complaint into the judicial arena. Once upon a time, behavioral health practitioners' occasional defamatory comments were limited to verbal conversations and handwritten documents (for example, a letter or note sent to a third party). In contrast, online and digital technology has expanded exponentially the ways in which defamatory comments can be communicated. Within minutes, a single online post, email message, or text message can go viral; once they click "send," practitioners lose all control over that message's digital destinations.

Defamation occurs when individuals make false statements that injure the reputation of another party and expose him or her to public contempt, hatred, ridicule, or condemnation. Unpleasant, angry, and hurtful comments, whether made in person or electronically, do not necessarily rise to the level of defamation.

Defamation can take two forms: libel and slander. Libel occurs when the communication is in written form—for example, in a letter, note, Facebook posting, email message, text message, or tweet about a colleague. Slander occurs when the communication is in oral form—for example, when a practitioner makes demeaning and derogatory comments about a colleague. This might occur during a Skype or Zoom call online.

In the digital age, behavioral health professionals can be legally liable for defamation of character if they post online comments or send messages electronically about a colleague that have the following three elements: (1) the allegations about the colleague were untrue; (2) the practitioner knew or should have known that the comments were untrue; and (3) the comments caused some injury to the colleague.

Practitioners' defamatory statements about colleagues—for example, about their alleged incompetence, unethical conduct, or mental status—can cause the colleague emotional distress, damage the colleague's reputation, or cause financial harm by jeopardizing the colleague's career in some way. Ideally, practitioners would address workplace and colleague disputes constructively, thoughtfully, and face-to-face instead of airing their grievances electronically.

CHAPTER THREE

Ethical, Regulatory, and Practice Standards

THE PROLIFERATION OF technology in behavioral health has led to several prominent efforts to develop ethics, regulatory, and practice standards that have compelling implications for individual practitioners and social service agencies.

ETHICAL STANDARDS

Since psychology's and social work's formal inauguration in the late 19th century, these original behavioral health professions have developed increasingly sophisticated and comprehensive ethical standards (Banks, 2012; Barsky, 2017, 2019; Reamer, 2013a, 2015, 2017, 2018a, 2018b). The mental health and marriage and family therapy professions have also developed comprehensive codes of ethics (Corey, Corey, & Corey, 2019; Knapp, VandeCreek, & Fingerhut, 2017). Recently, these codes have added standards pertaining to practitioners' use of technology to serve and communicate with clients.

The social work profession's efforts to update its code of ethics to address technology issues have been particularly ambitious. In 2015, NASW appointed a task force to determine whether changes were needed in its Code of Ethics to address concerns related to the use of technology.[1] In 2017, NASW adopted a revised code that includes extensive technology-related additions pertaining to informed consent, competent practice, conflicts of interest, privacy and confidentiality, sexual relationships, sexual harassment, interruption of services, unethical conduct of colleagues, supervision and consultation, education and training, client records, and evaluation and research. The code updates require social workers:

- To discuss with clients policies concerning use of technology in the provision of professional services. Social workers should explain to clients the ways in which social workers use technology to deliver services, communicate with clients, search for information about clients online, and store sensitive information about clients.

- Who plan to use technology in the provision of services to obtain client consent to the use of technology at the beginning of the professional-client relationship.

- Who use technology to communicate with clients to assess each client's capacity to provide informed consent.

- To verify the identity and location of clients they serve remotely (especially in case there is an emergency and to enable social workers to comply with laws in the client's jurisdiction).

- To assess clients' ability to access and use technology, particularly for online and remote services. Social workers should help clients identify alternate methods of service delivery if the use of technology to deliver services is not appropriate.

- To obtain client consent before conducting an online search for information about clients, as a way to respect clients' privacy (unless there are emergency or other compelling circumstances).

- To understand the special communication challenges associated with electronic and remote service delivery and how to address these challenges.

- Who use technology to comply with the laws of both the jurisdiction where the social worker is regulated and located and where the client is located (given that social workers and clients might be in different states or countries).

- To be aware of, assess, and respond to cultural, environmental, economic, disability, linguistic, and other social diversity issues that may affect delivery or use of services.

---

1   The author served on the NASW Code of Ethics task force that drafted revisions adopted in 2017.

- To not use technology to communicate with clients for personal or non-work-related purposes, in order to maintain appropriate boundaries.

- To take reasonable steps to prevent client access to social workers' personal social networking sites and personal technology, to avoid boundary confusion and inappropriate dual relationships.

- To be aware that posting personal information on professional websites or other media could cause boundary confusion, inappropriate dual relationships, or harm to clients.

- To be aware that clients may discover personal information about them based on their personal affiliations and use of social media.

- To avoid accepting requests from or engaging in personal relationships with clients on online social networks or other electronic media.

- To take reasonable steps (such as use of encryption, firewalls, and secure passwords) to protect the confidentiality of electronic communications, including information provided to clients or third parties.

- To develop and disclose policies and procedures for notifying clients of any breach of confidential information in a timely manner.

- To inform clients of unauthorized access to the social worker's electronic communication or storage systems (for example, cloud storage).

- To develop and inform clients about their policies on the use of electronic technology to gather information about clients.

- To avoid posting any identifying or confidential information about clients on professional websites or other forms of social media.

- Who use technology to facilitate evaluation or research to obtain clients' informed consent for the use of such technology. Social workers should assess clients' ability to use the technology and, when appropriate, offer reasonable alternatives.

Other behavioral health professions have also added standards related to practitioners' use of technology. For example, the American Counseling Association (2014) code of ethics now includes standards addressing counselors' electronic interactions with clients that are sexual in nature (standard A.5.c); nonprofessional electronic relationship with former clients (standard A.6.e); online supervision (standard F.2.c); and supervisors' electronic relationships with supervisees that are sexual in nature (standard F.3.b). The National Board for Certified Counselors (2016a) code of ethics includes standards addressing counselors' obligation to ensure the security of electronic records (standard 6); ensure clients' safety when counselors provide services remotely (standard 12); and comply with relevant licensing requirements when providing services electronically (standard 13). The American

Association for Marriage and Family Therapy (2015) code of ethics includes standards that address therapists' obligation to comply with laws pertaining to services provided electronically; assess the appropriateness of electronic services; inform clients of possible benefits and risks of electronic services; ensure the security of electronic communications and records; and develop skills to ensure skilled delivery of electronic services (standards 6.1 and 6.4).

It is particularly important that behavioral health professionals in the United States adhere to technology-related standards in their respective codes of ethics. Because these codes are widely recognized nationally, practitioners are held to their standards, even if they are not members of their national association that formally adopted the code. In litigation cases, codes of ethics are routinely introduced as evidence of the profession's standards of care, even when a practitioner who is a party in the litigation is not a member of the profession's national association. Further, many behavioral health licensing statutes and regulations in the United States draw on relevant codes of ethics, in whole or in part, and hold licensed practitioners to them, even if they are not members of the profession's national association (Reamer, 2015).

REGULATORY STANDARDS

In addition to new ethics standards, many behavioral health licensing bodies are adopting new regulatory standards related to technology. Developments in the social work profession are illustrative. Recognizing the profound impact that technology is having on social work practice, in 2013 the Association of Social Work Boards (ASWB) board of directors appointed an international task force to develop model regulatory standards for technology and social work practice.[2] ASWB embarked on development of new technology standards in response to demand from social work regulatory bodies around the globe for guidance concerning social workers' evolving use of technology. The ASWB task force included representatives from prominent social work practice, regulation, and education organizations throughout the world.

---

2   The Association of Social Work Boards is an international body composed of licensing and regulatory bodies in all 50 U.S. states, the District of Columbia, the U.S. Virgin Islands, Guam, the Northern Mariana Islands, and all 10 Canadian provinces. The author chaired the international task force sponsored by ASWB to develop model regulatory standards pertaining to social workers' use of technology.

The task force sought to develop standards for social workers who use digital and other electronic technology to provide information to the public, deliver services to clients, communicate with and about clients, manage confidential information and case records, and store and access information about clients. The group developed model standards addressing seven key concepts: practitioner competence; informed consent; privacy and confidentiality; boundaries, dual relationships, and conflicts of interest; records and documentation; collegial relationships; and social work practice across jurisdictional boundaries. These model standards are now influencing the development of licensing and regulatory laws around the world.

PRACTICE STANDARDS

In addition to pertinent ethical and regulatory standards, behavioral health professions have developed practice standards related to technology use. The social work profession's efforts have been particularly ambitious. In 2017, following unprecedented collaboration among key social work organizations in the United States—the National Association of Social Workers, Association of Social Work Boards, Council on Social Work Education, and Clinical Social Work Association—the profession formally adopted new, comprehensive practice standards focused on social workers' and social work educators' use of technology (NASW et al., 2017).[3] Approved by these respective organizations' boards of directors, these transformational, comprehensive standards address a wide range of compelling issues related to social workers' use of technology. The standards include four major sections: (1) provision of information to the public; (2) designing and delivering services; (3) gathering, managing, and storing information; and (4) social work education and supervision.

- *Provision of information to the public*: This section summarizes core ethical issues involving social workers' use of technology. It also states that social workers who use technology to provide information to the public shall take reasonable steps to ensure the accuracy and validity of the information they disseminate.

- *Designing and delivering services*: This section states that social workers who provide electronic social work services shall comply with the laws and regulations that govern electronic social work services within both

---

3   The author chaired this national task forced charged with developing practice standards related to social workers' use of technology.

the jurisdiction in which the social worker is located and in which the client is located; understand, comply, and stay current with any and all laws that govern the provision of social work services and inform clients of the social worker's legal obligations, just as they would when providing services in person; inform the client of relevant benefits and risks of services provided electronically; obtain and maintain the knowledge and skills required to do so in a safe, competent, and ethical manner; establish and maintain confidentiality policies and procedures consistent with relevant statutes, regulations, rules, and ethical standards; take reasonable steps to ensure that business associates (for example, those who process social workers' insurance claims) use proper encryption and have confidentiality policies and procedures consistent with social work standards and relevant laws; maintain clear professional boundaries in their relationships with clients; develop a social media policy that they share with clients; consider the implications of their use of personal mobile phones and other electronic communication devices for work purposes; plan for the possibility that electronic services will be interrupted unexpectedly; be familiar with emergency services in the jurisdiction where the client is located and share this information with clients; refrain from soliciting electronic or online testimonials from clients or former clients who, because of their particular circumstances, are vulnerable to undue influence; and use technology responsibly in conjunction with organizing and advocacy efforts, fundraising, agency administration, supervision, consultation, and program evaluation and research.

- *Gathering, managing, and storing information*: This section states that social workers who provide electronic social work services shall explain to clients whether and how they intend to use electronic devices or communication technologies to gather, manage, and store client information; ensure clear delineation between personal and professional communications and information when social workers gather, manage, and store client information electronically; take reasonable steps to ensure that confidential information concerning clients or research participants is gathered, managed, and stored in a secure manner and in accordance with relevant federal and state statutes, regulations, and organizational policies; take reasonable steps to develop and implement policies regarding which personnel have access to clients' electronic records, keeping in mind the value of limiting access to those colleagues who truly require it; develop and disclose policies and procedures concerning how they would notify clients of any breach of their confidential records; shall gather information for social work practice or research in a manner that reasonably ensures its reliability and accuracy; take reasonable steps to protect the confidentiality of information that is shared with other parties electronically; ensure that client access to electronic records is provided in a manner that takes client confidentiality, privacy, and the client's best interests into account; not gather information about clients from online sources without the client's consent, except for compelling professional reasons; respect colleagues and verify the accuracy of information before using information gathered online about colleagues; treat colleagues with respect and represent accurately and fairly the qualifications, views, and obligations of colleagues when social workers communicate using electronic tools; be aware of how information that is posted or stored electronically for use by others may be used and interpreted, and take reasonable steps to ensure that the information is accurate, respectful, and complete; develop and follow appropriate policies regarding whether and how they can access electronic client records remotely; and take steps to protect their clients, employer, themselves, and the environment when an electronic device is no longer needed, is phased out, or is outdated.

- *Social work education and supervision*: This section states that social workers who use technology to design and deliver education and training shall develop competence in the ethical use of the technology in a manner appropriate for the particular context; provide information to students and practitioners about the ethical use of technology, including potential benefits and risks; examine and keep current with relevant emerging knowledge related to the use of technology in social work practice; provide students with social media policies to provide them with guidance about ethical considerations; provide clear guidance on professional expectations when evaluating students on their use of technology and how assignments will be graded; provide students with information about how to manage technological problems that may be caused by loss of power, viruses, hardware failures, lost or stolen devices, or other issues that may disrupt the educational process; ensure that practitioners and students have sufficient understanding of the cultural, social, and legal contexts of the other locations where the practitioners or students are located; ensure that students have sufficient access to technological support to assist with technological questions or problems that may arise during the educational process; take appropriate measures to promote academic standards related to honesty, integrity, freedom of expression, and respect for the dignity and worth of all people when using technology for educational purposes; take precautions to ensure maintenance of appropriate educator–student boundaries during electronic interactions; and ensure that supervisors who use technology to provide supervision are able to assess students' and supervisees' learning and professional competence.

Along with technology-related standards in the NASW Code of Ethics, these widely endorsed and recognized practice standards are used in licensing board cases and lawsuits when questions surface about whether social workers used technology ethically and responsibly. In this regard, all behavioral health professionals should be familiar with recognized practice standards adopted by their respective professional associations and adhere to them when they use technology to communicate with clients, deliver services to them remotely, post information online, and manage client records.

CHAPTER FOUR

Challenges in Integrated Health and Behavioral Health Education Settings

ONE OF THE most encouraging developments in behavioral health is the advent of integrated care. The core feature of this model involves recognizing and addressing the complex connections between physical and mental health—a phenomenon well understood by behavioral health professionals, who have always appreciated the intimate connection between mind and body.

CHALLENGES IN INTEGRATED HEALTH SETTINGS

In recent years, behavioral health professionals have grown to appreciate the need to integrate physical health and behavioral health services. Health care professionals—including physicians, physician assistants, nurse practitioners, nurses, pharmacists, and physical therapists, among others—understand how their patients' behavioral health challenges can affect their physical health. Similarly, behavioral health professionals understand the ways in which clients' physical health challenges can affect their emotional well-being.

Although the proliferation of integrated health care settings is a relatively recent phenomenon, the concept is not new. In the United States, in the 1930s some settings created what were known as multispecialty group practices in which primary and specialty care practitioners shared common governance, infrastructure, finances, and patients. In the 1970s, health maintenance organizations emerged, in which practitioners from diverse health and behavioral health professions integrated care under one roof or in networks in an effort to coordinate care and provide services in a cost-effective manner (Collins et al., 2010; Curtis & Christian, 2012; Horevitz & Manoleas, 2013).

Many health care historians assert that the first truly integrated behavioral health program was the Gouverneur Health Program, which began in the 1970s in New York City, although the model did not begin to flourish until the 1990s. In the early 2000s, the U.S. military and the Health Resources and Services Administration (HRSA)—the primary federal agency for improving health equity—promoted the model. In the private sector, Health Partners in Minneapolis and Sharp Health in San Diego helped put integrated behavioral health on the map. A key by-product of the Patient Protection and Affordable Care Act was creation of the federal Academy for Integrating Behavioral Health and Primary Care, whose mission is to help build behavioral health care into primary care throughout the United States (Collins et al., 2010).

Behavioral health professionals applaud the emergence and maturation of integrated care. However, one challenging by-product of this integration concerns protection of clients' private and confidential information stored in electronic health records (Reamer, 2018f). The following are several examples:

- A mental health center in a rural community has a primary care practice on site; clients receive medical care from internists, physician assistants, pharmacists, nurse practitioners, and nurses. A mental health counselor's client was being treated in the health practice for diabetes and hepatitis C. The practitioner provided supportive mental health counseling. The client is in recovery from opiate addiction. The client disclosed to the counselor that he is struggling with sexual orientation issues. The client told the counselor he would prefer to keep this information private, because he knows several clinic staffers socially; the client asked the counselor not to share these details with his primary health care providers. However, the electronic health record allows the primary health care staffers to access all of the social counselor's notes.

- A neighborhood health clinic serves a large low-income community. About a year ago the clinic hired two full-time social workers to provide mental health services to clinic patients. A 16-year-old patient received medical care for a sexually transmitted infection (STI). The teen also received mental health counseling for anxiety symptoms. The teen told his clinic physician that he was embarrassed about the STI and did not want the social worker to know about it. However, the social worker had full access to the teen's electronic health record.

- A large health maintenance organization (HMO) provides enrolled patients with comprehensive health care, including primary care, behavioral health, orthopedics, dermatology, podiatry, ophthalmology, optometry, ob-gyn, gastroenterology, and rheumatology, among other specialty services. A group of social workers at the HMO became concerned that all staffers had access to the social workers' behavioral health care notes. They arranged to meet with senior administrators to express their concern that HMO staffers who ordinarily would have no reason to access social workers' clinical notes had viewed them.

The proliferation of integrated behavioral health programs that rely on electronic health records has led to vigorous discussion about ways to protect the privacy and confidentiality of behavioral health practitioners' clients. It is important for practitioners to encourage development of meaningful and practical protocols consistent with prevailing ethical standards. A key resource for practitioners is the Center for Integrated Health Solutions, a collaboration between the federal Substance Abuse and Mental Health Services Administration and the Health Resources and Services Administration. The center provides behavioral health and health care professionals with a rich array of resources designed to promote integrated care. Among these resources is a guide to pertinent confidentiality issues.

Behavioral health professionals who are employed in integrated settings should be mindful of several key guidelines when they make decisions about documentation and disclosure of sensitive information. First, they should understand fully which colleagues can and should access their clinical notes. This may influence practitioners' judgments about the extent to which they include sensitive information in their notes. Second, practitioners should consult with appropriate administrators about establishing protocols, possibly including firewalls, to ensure that only staffers who have a need to know have access to practitioners' clinical notes. Third, practitioners should ensure that clients understand who will have access to information about their behavioral health counseling (consistent with the ethical principle of informed consent). Finally, practitioners should ensure that their agencies comply with relevant federal and state confidentiality laws (including HIPAA and 42 CFR Part 2 at the federal level and various health care confidentiality laws at the state level) and pertinent standards in practitioners' respective codes of ethics, primarily related to confidentiality.

EDUCATING STUDENTS AND PRACTITIONERS

When professional education in counseling and social work was inaugurated in the late nineteenth century, technology consisted primarily of the telephone, which at that point was only twenty years old. Students who enrolled during the Great Depression in the 1930s were introduced to a new form of technology that, as it evolved, transformed their ability to produce written work: the electric typewriter. Practitioners who completed their degrees during the turbulent 1960s were able to send "facsimiles" using the first commercially available fax machines, and in the 1970s they analyzed research data recorded and programmed on punch cards that they fed through massive card reading machines. By the 1980s students in the behavioral health professions were able to leave messages for their field-internship clients on widely available answering machines.

In contrast, contemporary students in behavioral health education programs take courses online; some never set foot in a physical classroom. Their internship supervisor may communicate with them using a video link from hundreds or thousands of miles away. Students may post comments in online chat rooms and converse with fellow students and faculty members they never meet in person. Similarly, many practitioners enroll in online seminars and courses for educational purposes and to fulfill their continuing education requirements set forth by their licensing board.

As noted above, many of the technology practice standards adopted jointly by the National Association of Social Workers, Association of Social Work Boards, Council on Social Work Education, and Clinical Social Work Association focus explicitly on professional education, including undergraduate and graduate education, staff development, supervision, and continuing education (NASW et al., 2017). These are among the most ambitious in the behavioral health professions. The standards have significant implications for educators' efforts to comply with the Council on Social Work Education's (2015) *Educational Policy and Accreditation Standards* that pertain to technology: "Social workers ... understand emerging forms of technology and the ethical use of technology in social work practice" (p. 7). The standards focus on core issues related to competencies in the use of technology for educational purposes; academic standards and integrity; training social workers in the use of technology to serve clients; and social work supervision (practice-based supervision and field education).

Current standards state that behavioral health professionals who use technology to design and deliver clinical education, training, and supervision must develop competence in the ethical use of the technology through appropriate study and training (Fange et al., 2014; Goldingay & Boddy, 2017; Phelan, 2015; Sawrikar et al., 2015). They must examine the extent to which professional education provided using technology enables students to master core professional skills and engage in appropriate education, study, training, consultation, and supervision with professionals who are competent in the use of technology-mediated tools for educational purposes (Siebert, Siebert, & Spaulding-Givens, 2013).

Prominent research suggests a number of best practices for online or distance teaching that should be reflected in professional education, including continuing education required by behavioral health licensing boards (Boettcher & Conrad, 2016; Ko & Rossen, 2017; Reeves & Reeves, 2008). Educators who use technology to teach knowledge and skills should anticipate the possibility that some students will have special needs that require use of technology-based adaptive devices that enhance access (Sawrikar et al., 2015). Educators who teach online and distance courses must take these factors into account and, to the extent feasible, incorporate reasonable accommodations (Duncan-Daston et al., 2013; Fange et al., 2014; Sawrikar et al., 2015).

The Universal Design for Learning Guidelines provides behavioral health educators with state-of-the-art protocols to enhance accessibility of technology-based instruction (National Center on User Design for Learning, 2018). These guidelines address issues related to student engagement, perception, self-regulation, comprehension, language and symbols, physical action, expression, and communication. It is especially important that behavioral health professionals who use technology to teach students in remote locations ensure that they have sufficient understanding of the cultural, social, and legal contexts of the locations where the students and practitioners are located. For example, online instructors must keep in mind that state laws differ considerably with regard to exceptions to clients' confidentiality rights (for example, mandatory reporting and duty to disclose confidential information to protect third parties from harm) and informed consent (for example, minors' right to consent to treatment without notification of parents by behavioral health practitioners).

Curricula that teach students and practitioners about ways to use technology must include state-of-the-art knowledge about effective and ethical use of technology (Goldingay & Boddy, 2017). It is especially important to address whether and when technology is an appropriate way to assess clients' clinical needs, provide services, communicate with clients, and locate information about clients. Educators must teach about ways to develop protocols to evaluate client outcomes and to think critically about the potential benefits and risks of using technology to serve clients. Practitioners who develop these skills before using technology to serve clients may reduce the risk of licensing board complaints and lawsuits.

For behavioral health educators whose courses include substantial online components or are entirely remote, current research suggests a number of best practices for teaching that should be incorporated (Boettcher & Conrad, 2016; Ko & Rossen, 2017; Reamer, 2019; Reeves & Reeves, 2008). According to these authors, educators should draw on these best practices to comply with widely accepted standards. These include:

- *Maintaining a strong and consistent presence at the course site:* Research evidence suggests that the most effective online learning occurs when instructors are present on the course site multiple times per week—ideally daily (Bentley, Secret, & Cummings, 2015; Dixson, 2010). Frequent comments, feedback, and postings by instructors send a message to students that their learning is a priority and that the instructors care about and are paying close attention to them. Students can become frustrated when they sense that instructors are not engaged in the course on a regular basis. Of course, this expectation can be burdensome and time-consuming for instructors. Instructors who anticipate that they will not be available for a period of time, perhaps due to personal or family issues, would do well to alert students in advance. Instructors can keep students in the loop in a variety of ways, including posting comments and announcements on online discussion boards and faculty blogs.

- *Creating a supportive online community:* As in face-to-face teaching in traditional classrooms, in online teaching it is important to facilitate supportive connections among students. This enhances opportunity for peer-informed learning and consultation, and minimizes the likelihood that students will feel alone, isolated, or abandoned. One practical strategy is to design assignments that require students to engage and communicate with each other through online comments and dialogues. Organizing students into small groups for particular activities can be useful.

- *Developing a set of explicit expectations for students:* Instructors should spell out in considerable detail what they expect from students when courses include significant online activities and assignments. Key topics include tasks to be completed, timelines for completion of assignments and posting of comments, and the amount of time students are expected to devote to the course on a weekly basis. In addition, instructors should share with students what they can expect from faculty. Key topics include frequency and scheduling of instructors' comments, schedule of virtual office hours, availability by email or phone, and the nature of website monitoring.

- *Using a variety of teaching techniques and experiences:* As in courses that are taught solely face-to-face, students who participate in online behavioral health education typically appreciate a mix of teaching approaches and learning opportunities. These may include assigning tasks to be completed solo, small-group projects, activities to be worked on in pairs, online readings, video presentations, webcasts, videos, and audio recordings.

- *Using synchronous and asynchronous learning activities:* Currently available software and course management systems enable instructors and students to meet in "real time," schedules permitting. Many students find such in-the-moment, live presentations and discussions—known as synchronous instruction—particularly compelling and valuable. Along with synchronous teaching and learning, it is appropriate for instructors to set aside time for asynchronous activities, where students read, reflect, and post comments on their own schedules.

- *Soliciting feedback from students throughout the course:* Behavioral health professionals have long known the importance of checking in with clients about their experience with the services they are receiving; periodic monitoring is an essential element of behavioral health practice. The same concept applies to courses that are taught primarily or exclusively online. This is especially important given the remote (geographical) connection between instructor and student. As educators have known since time immemorial, students have different learning styles and preferences with regard to didactic presentation, experiential exercises, group projects, and writing.

  Online teaching introduces an additional challenge, given the unique and, for many students, novel way to learn. Many students are experiencing virtual lectures, online chat rooms, webcasts, uploads, downloads, podcasts, livestreaming, and other features of contemporary learning management systems for the first time. Some embrace this approach to learning and some struggle with it, or at least certain of its elements. Thus, it is vitally important for instructors to take students' educational temperature periodically to assess what is working and what is not, and to adjust or accommodate accordingly. Inviting student feedback at the end of the course, which is standard practice in many in-person courses, is too late and turns the feedback into a postmortem assessment or academic autopsy.

- *Preparing discussion posts that invite students' responses, questions, observations, and reflections:* Instructors must be diligent in their efforts to engage students in active dialogue. This is especially important given that students' online comments provide the primary, perhaps only, way for instructors to know their students well if there is limited or no face-to-face contact. One advantage of asynchronous online discussion and posts is that, in contrast to synchronous online and classroom discussions, students have time to reflect and compose their thoughts.

- *Combining core concept learning with customized and personalized learning:* The most effective teaching provides students with opportunities to apply these concepts to their unique areas of interest. For example, online instruction focused on cultural and social diversity in behavioral health might provide a student who is interested in the delivery of social services to older adults with an opportunity to do a web-based video presentation on the ways in which different cultural and ethnic groups understand the concept of aging and end-of-life challenges, conceptualize the role of families and nursing homes in caregiving, and have access to important social services.

A number of prominent technology standards focus explicitly on supervision and field or internship instruction (NASW et al., 2017). Some behavioral health supervisors and internship instructors are communicating with supervisees remotely, either as supplements to face-to-face meetings or exclusively remotely. According to current standards, behavioral health professionals who use technology to provide supervision must ensure that they are able to assess students' and supervisees' learning and professional competence (Maidment, 2006). This, too, is a practical way for supervisors to reduce the risk of licensing board complaints and litigation that raises questions about the quality of their supervision.

Some behavioral health regulatory guidelines also include standards pertaining to remote supervision. For example, the Association of Marital and Family Therapy Regulatory Boards (2016) teletherapy guidelines explicitly address practitioners' obligation to develop competencies to enable them to supervise remotely, adhere to relevant state licensing board requirements related to supervision, and inform supervisees of potential benefits and risks associated with remote supervision (Guideline 20).

In addition, several behavioral health codes of ethics include standards pertaining to remote supervision. For example, the American Counseling Association (2014) code of ethics states, "When using technology in supervision, counselor supervisors are competent in the use of those technologies. Supervisors take the necessary precautions to protect the confidentiality of all information transmitted through any electronic means" (standard F.2.c.).

Further, clinical supervisors and internship instructors should take reasonable steps to ensure that they are able to assess students' and supervisees' learning and professional competence and provide appropriate feedback. Behavioral health professionals who supervise remotely should acquaint themselves with guidelines concerning provision of remote supervision adopted by the jurisdiction(s) in which the supervisors and supervisees live and practice.

CHAPTER FIVE

Preventing and Managing Risk

ALONG WITH THEIR benefits, behavioral health professionals' increasing use of digital and other technology to provide distance services and communicate with clients increases potential risks to clients and practitioners. Improper or unethical use of this technology can expose clients to harm as a result of inadequate informed consent procedures; privacy and confidentiality breaches; mismanaged boundaries and dual relationships; conflicts of interest; practitioner incompetence; inadequate recordkeeping and documentation; improper termination of services; and mistreatment of colleagues (Klein, 2011). Further, practitioners' improper or unethical use of digital technology can expose them to the risk of litigation and allegations of professional misconduct.

Risk management is a broad term that refers to efforts to protect clients, practitioners, and employers (Carroll, 2011). In behavioral health, risk management includes protection of clients and the prevention of ethics complaints (for example, filed with national behavioral health associations), lawsuits, and licensing board complaints filed against practitioners. Ethics complaints filed with national behavioral health associations typically allege violation of the organization's code of ethics. Lawsuits allege professional malpractice; licensing board complaints allege violation of standards of practice set forth in licensing laws and regulations. Lawsuits can result in monetary judgments against practitioners; licensing board complaints can result in fines, revocation or suspension of a professional license, probation, mandated supervision and continuing education, reprimand, or censure. Ethics complaints filed with national behavioral health associations can result in sanctions or corrective action.

Professional malpractice is generally considered a form of negligence. The concept applies to professionals who are required to perform in a manner consistent with the legal concept of the standard of care in the profession—that is, the way a reasonable and prudent professional should act under the same or similar circumstances (Bernstein & Hartsell, 2004; Reamer, 2015). That is, behavioral health professionals who use technology to communicate with clients, deliver services, and manage and store information must adhere to current standards of care in the profession, as reflected in the prominent codes of ethics, widely recognized practice standards, federal and state laws, and relevant literature.

In the United States, the concept of standard of care emerged in a key court ruling in 1896. Although the landmark case, *Coombs v. Beede*, did not involve behavioral health, the legal principles and guidelines established by this case are particularly relevant to contemporary practitioners' use of technology to serve clients.

The court case concerned a protracted dispute between an architect, George Coombs, and his client, Clarence Beede, who retained Coombs to prepare architectural plans for a house in the city of Lewiston, Maine. Beede claimed that Coombs' plans were not consistent with Beede's explicit instructions and, as a result, he did not pay Coombs' invoice for services rendered. Coombs, in contrast, claimed he fulfilled his professional duty to Beede and filed a lawsuit to recover payment.

In its fine-grained analysis, the Maine Supreme Court explored the essential elements of professional duty when a practitioner enters into a relationship with a client. In its formally published and oft-cited opinion, the court wrote:

> In an examination of the merits of the controversy between these parties, we must bear in mind that the plaintiff [architect Coombs] was not a contractor who had entered into an agreement to construct a house for the defendant [owner Beede], but was merely an agent of the defendant to assist him in building one. The responsibility resting on an architect is essentially the same as that which rests upon the lawyer to his client, or upon the physician to his patient, or which rests on anyone to another where such person pretends to possess some skill and ability in some special employment, and offers his services to the public on account of his fitness to act in the line of business for which he may be employed. The undertaking of an architect implies that he possesses skill and ability, including taste, sufficient to enable him to perform the required services at least ordinarily and reasonably well; and that

he will exercise and apply in the given case his skill and ability, his judgment and taste, reasonably and without neglect. (*Coombs v. Beede* 36A 104 [1896] Supreme Court, Maine)

More than a century later, this conceptual framework continues to be applied in contemporary cases across all professions where there is a legal dispute about the extent to which a professional was negligent in the delivery of services to clients. In recent years, resolution of disputes involving behavioral health professionals' use of technology has rested on recently adopted standards of care. That is, courts of law and behavioral health licensing boards typically seek to determine how a reasonable and prudent practitioner, with the same or similar education, would have used technology to communicate with clients, deliver services, and manage and store information.

Malpractice in behavioral health usually is the result of a practitioner's active violation of a client's rights (in legal terms, acts of commission, misfeasance, or malfeasance) or a practitioner's failure to perform certain duties (known as acts of omission or nonfeasance). Misfeasance is customarily defined as the commission of a proper act in a wrongful or injurious manner, or the improper performance of an act that might have been performed lawfully. For example, ordinarily it is proper for a behavioral health practitioner to use technology to communicate with clients remotely and provide services to them without meeting them in person, so long as the practitioner complies with current ethical, regulatory, and practice standards. Misfeasance occurs when a practitioner makes mistakes using technology—for example, by using software that does not adequately protect clients' privacy or by inadvertently entering inaccurate information in a client's electronic record.

Malfeasance is ordinarily defined as the commission of a wrongful or unlawful act. Examples include a behavioral health practitioner who exchanges "sexting" messages with a client or who knowingly enters fraudulent information in the client's electronic record.

Nonfeasance is defined as the failure to perform a duty that one ought to have performed. Examples include a practitioner who neglects to obtain a client's fully informed consent prior to providing services to the client remotely, or who fails to provide the client with information about what to do in the event of a clinical emergency that the practitioner is unable to address remotely (for example, when there is a risk of suicide and the client lives in a distant community).

Some malpractice and liability claims result from genuine mistakes or inadvertent oversight on the part of behavioral health professionals (for example, a practitioner sends an email message containing confidential information to the wrong recipient or makes documentation errors in an electronic health record). Here are case examples:

A counseling psychologist in private (independent) practice provided counseling services to a 22-year-old college student who struggled with clinical depression and had a history of suicidal ideation. The student graduated from the local college and moved back home, to another state, to live with his parents. The client and psychologist agreed to continue the counseling long distance, using Skype. Unfortunately, the client committed suicide. The deceased client's parents sued the psychologist, alleging that the clinician should not have agreed to provide distance counseling, given the client's known suicide risk. The fact that the psychologist used Skype, which is not HIPAA compliant, and was not licensed in the client's home state were key issues in the litigation, among others.

A school social worker provided counseling to five middle school students who struggled with social skills. The social worker decided to begin a social skills group and drafted an email message to his individual clients explaining the group's goals, schedule, and format. The email message invited the students to enroll in the group. The social worker entered each student's email address in the "To" field of the outgoing email message without realizing that this would enable each recipient to see the name of the social worker's other clients. One of the recipients was very upset that her fellow students learned that she was in counseling, and she mentioned this to her parents. The parents were enraged at the social worker's breach of their daughter's confidentiality. Coincidentally, the student's mother was a malpractice attorney. The parents sued the social worker for negligence and filed a licensing board complaint.

A mental health counselor employed in a group psychotherapy practice provided counseling to a 14-year-old client who struggled with sexual orientation issues. The client felt rejected by his parents, whose religious views rejected homosexuality, and talked to the counselor about wanting to run away from home. The counselor helped the client process his feelings and discussed the risks associated with running away from home.

On several occasions, the client and counselor exchanged text messages. Late one night, the client sent the counselor a text message that read: "I really need to talk to u. I can't live here anymore. My parents tell me I'm going to hell because I'm gay. I'm not sure I want to live. I just don't know if I'm going to make it."

Unfortunately, the counselor did not see the text message. The following morning, the counselor went away with his family on vacation and had a colleague cover his caseload for him. The next day, the client committed suicide. The parents sued the counselor, alleging that the counselor failed to manage their son's suicide risk properly. The parents' lawyer was able to access their son's text messages and read the distress message the client had sent the counselor. The lawsuit claimed that the counselor failed to have a protocol in place to respond to clinically relevant text messages and failed to ensure that the colleague who covered for him had access to the client's text messages, which were not documented in the client's electronic record accessed by the counselor's colleague.

Other malpractice claims ensue from a deliberate decision (for example, a behavioral health professional engages with a client online on a social networking site or decides to divulge confidential information about a client who sent a threatening email message in order to protect a third party who was mentioned in the message). Here are several case examples that raise potential risk-management issues:

A mental health counselor employed at a residential substance use treatment program planned to start a part-time independent (private) practice. A colleague informed her of a company that is recruiting clinicians to offer remote counseling services using its online platform. The company's primary service offers counseling services entirely via text messages. Clients can opt to exchange text messages with a clinician to address challenges in their lives, without any in-person, video, or telephone contact. The counselor was unsure about whether this text-based treatment model meets prevailing clinical and ethical standards in mental health counseling.

A marriage and family therapist was the clinical director at a mental health center located in a large rural state. Many of the agency's clients live in remote areas that require lengthy drives to receive behavioral health services. In an effort to enhance the agency's reach to the state's rural locations, and to minimize travel burdens for clients, the clinical director and her staffers considered inaugurating an avatar-based counseling model, which they had heard a conference presenter discuss. The model invites all counseling participants—clinicians and clients—to create avatars, which are graphic representations of themselves. Participants log into the agency's website and their avatars interact with each other during individual and group counseling sessions. The clinical director and her colleagues were intrigued about the avatar model and wanted to explore the clinical and ethical implications.

A psychiatrist was the director of an outpatient psychiatric clinic operated by a large hospital. The hospital, which included a broad array of medical specialties and clinics, recently developed an online portal that allowed patients to access their records remotely. The psychiatrist was concerned about allowing patients to view hospital staffers' behavioral health notes outside of the presence of their clinician. The psychiatrist was concerned that some patients might misinterpret the contents of their behavioral health notes and could be harmed emotionally. The psychiatrist also had some concerns about the quality of some of her staffers' documentation skills and worried that making their notes available to clients without careful screening beforehand by a supervisor could expose the hospital and its staffers to risk.

A behavioral health professional's unethical behavior or misconduct (for example, engaging in an inappropriate and salacious online relationship with a former client) also can trigger malpractice claims. Here are several case examples:

A mental health counselor directed the behavioral health program at a school for adolescents with special needs. One of her clients was a 17-year-old student who was diagnosed with clinical depression and anxiety. Over time, the counselor—a married mother—began to exchange informal text messages that became increasingly informal and affectionate. The counselor and client began a sexual relationship, which the student's parents discovered after scrolling through text messages on their son's smartphone. Several text messages included sexually explicit content. The parents sued the counselor and filed a licensing board complaint against her. During legal proceedings, the text messages were introduced as formal evidence against the counselor.

A clinical psychologist provided counseling services at an outpatient behavioral health clinic that specialized in treatment of trauma victims. Many of the psychologist's clients were victims of domestic violence, sexual assault, and child abuse. Over time, the psychologist became sexually involved with four of his adult clients, all of whom filed lawsuits against the clinician. (The psychologist was also convicted in criminal court and sentenced to prison.) Evidence against the psychologist included incriminating email and text messages he exchanged with his victims (for example, electronic messages from the psychologist that expressed his affection for his victims and arranged liaisons with them).

A social worker at a community mental health center provided counseling to a woman who struggled with clinical depression and symptoms of borderline personality disorder. The client had been referred to the social worker by her cousin, who was the agency's office manager and close friends with the social worker.

The office manager was hospitalized following a suicide attempt. The office manager's mother took possession of the office manager's smartphone during the hospitalization. With the office manager's permission, the mother accessed her daughter's smartphone content in order to write down contact information for several of the office manager's friends, who wanted updates about her status. When the office manager's mother accessed the smartphone's content, she scrolled through her daughter's text messages and read a series of exchanges between the office manager and the social worker concerning the social worker's client, the office manager's cousin. Several of the messages clearly include gossip about the client, including harsh, critical comments about the client's hygiene, challenging personality, and trauma history. The agency office manager's mother told her relative, the client, about these messages. The client sued the social worker for violating her confidentiality.

In general, malpractice occurs when there is evidence that (1) at the time of the alleged malpractice, a legal duty existed between the practitioner and the client (for example, in Cases A, B, and C discussed in Chapter 2, the behavioral health professionals who provide distance clinical services would owe a duty to their clients, even if they never met them in person); (2) the practitioner was derelict in that duty, either through an omission or through an action that occurred (for example, if the psychologist in Case A failed to use proper informed consent procedures before embarking on a distance counseling relationship, failed to be available when needed, or failed to protect clients' electronically stored confidential information); (3) the client suffered some harm or injury (for example, if there is evidence that the client in Case B suffered emotional distress and required additional psychiatric care after the social worker who provided her with distance counseling services was not available in an emergency and did not provide the client with information about what to do in the event of an emergency); and (4) the professional's dereliction of duty was the direct and proximate cause of the harm or injury (for example, if there is evidence that the client in Case B suffered injuries as a direct result of the social worker's mismanagement of the distance counseling relationship).

In contrast, in licensing board cases, judgments against behavioral health professionals do not require evidence that their actions (commission) or inactions (omission) caused harm. Rather, practitioners can be sanctioned based simply on evidence that their conduct violated standards contained in licensing statutes and regulations. Here are several case examples:

A counseling psychologist in a rural community counseled adult clients in a mental health center. In her personal life, the psychologist was dating a man she met at her local gym. The couple moved in together and planned to marry. The psychologist learned from her partner that the partner's former girlfriend was harassing him and posting hostile online comments about his new relationship with the psychologist. The psychologist's partner's former girlfriend was an active client at the psychologist's mental health center, where she received counseling from one of the psychologist's colleagues.

The psychologist read the comments posted online by her partner's former girlfriend and became incensed. The psychologist posted angry comments online in response and sent her partner's former girlfriend a series of hostile text messages warning her to cease her online postings. The partner's former girlfriend knew that the psychologist was employed at the agency where the former girlfriend was a client. The partner's former girlfriend filed a licensing board complaint against the psychologist accusing her of boundary violations and engaging in a conflict of interest because of the psychologist's nonprofessional communications with a client who received services from the psychologist's agency. The licensing board sanctioned the psychologist, placed her on probation, and required her to obtain ethics consultation.

A mental health counselor managed a large government-sponsored program for veterans who were transitioning to civilian life. After a holiday party, the counselor sent an email message to staffers that some recipients claimed mocked veterans. The email message included photographs of a toy Christmas elf pleading for anxiety medication and hanging itself with an electrical cord. The counselor resigned her position and claimed that the email message and photographs were taken out of context and misinterpreted. The state licensing board suspended the counselor's license after finding evidence of a breach of professional conduct.

A clinical social worker in independent (private) practice provided counseling services to parents of a young child whose behavior was challenging. The parents owed the social worker a large amount of money for unpaid counseling fees. The social worker repeatedly asked the parents for payment, without success. The social worker sent the parents an email message that demanded payment and accused the parents of being "irresponsible," "greedy," "cruel," "deceitful," and "manipulative." The parents filed a licensing board complaint alleging that the social worker was unprofessional. The licensing board reprimanded the social worker for her "unprofessional conduct" and required her to get formal ethics consultation.

A school counselor was involved in a protracted workplace dispute with a colleague. After several months of conflict, the counselor sent an email message under an assumed name and bogus email address to the colleague's spouse, accusing the colleague of grossly unethical behavior that, the email message said, "you ought to know about." The counselor's colleague was appalled by the message and, after some forensic investigation, was able to document that the impersonated email message was sent by the counselor. The colleague filed a licensing board complaint against the counselor. The board suspended the counselor's license and, as a condition of reinstatement, required the counselor to seek professional consultation about her ethical misjudgment and enroll in a series of ethics-related continuing education courses.

Behavioral health professionals who use digital technology and provide distance counseling services can take a number of steps to protect clients and themselves (Reamer, 2013a). Although these steps cannot guarantee clear outcomes with which all practitioners agree—especially considering the ambiguity and controversy surrounding practitioners' use of digital technology—they can enhance practitioners' efforts to protect clients and themselves. The challenge for behavioral health professionals is to exercise good-faith judgment systematically while being mindful of the profession's time-honored ethical standards.

1. Consult colleagues. Behavioral health professionals who contemplate using digital and distance counseling tools should consult colleagues who have specialized knowledge or expertise related to these issues. Practitioners in private or independent practice should participate in peer consultation groups to discuss their use of distance counseling technology.

Behavioral health practitioners should continuously learn about changes in technology used to provide distance services. Competence depends on the type of technology and how it is used, and may include knowing how to communicate effectively while using the technology to provide behavioral health services; handle emergency situations from a remote location; apply the laws of both the practitioner's and client's location; be sensitive to the client's culture, including the client's cultural community and linguistic, social, and economic environment; attend to clients' unique needs and challenges; ensure that the technology is in working order to provide effective services and avoid disruption; keep abreast of the changing landscape of technology; and adapt accordingly.

Behavioral health professionals employed in settings that have ethics committees (committees that provide staffers with a forum for consultation on difficult cases), such as psychiatric hospitals or psychiatric units in general hospitals, should take advantage of this form of consultation when they face complicated ethical issues involving their use of technology (Reamer, 2013b). Moreover, practitioners who are sued or who are named in licensing board complaints can help demonstrate their competent decision-making skills by showing that they sought consultation.

2. Obtain appropriate supervision. Behavioral health professionals who have access to a supervisor should take full advantage of this opportunity. Supervisors may be able to help practitioners navigate complicated circumstances involving their use of digital and distance technology to provide services. Moreover, practitioners who are sued or named in a licensing board complaint can help demonstrate their competent decision-making skills by showing that they sought supervision related to technology use.

Supervisors should be sure to provide advice based on current knowledge and standards related to technology. Supervisors should document the supervision they provide. This can be very helpful if questions are raised about the quality of the supervision. In principle, under the legal doctrine of *respondeat superior* (Latin for "let the master respond") and what lawyers call vicarious liability, supervisors can be held responsible for negligent acts engaged in by their supervisees related to technology use. Problems can arise for supervisors if there is evidence that they provided advice that was not grounded in current standards of care related to the use of technology in behavioral health.

3. Review relevant ethical standards. It is vitally important that behavioral health professionals become familiar with and consult relevant codes of ethics, especially updates related to use of technology to deliver services and communicate with clients. They should pay particular attention to guidelines concerning ethical issues that often form the basis for malpractice claims and lawsuits—for example, confidentiality, informed consent, conflicts of interest, boundary issues and dual relationships, client records, defamation of character, and termination of services (Reamer, 2015).

In addition, code of ethics standards provide the basis for adjudication of ethics complaints filed against members of behavioral health associations; further, many state licensing boards and courts of law use codes of ethics, or portions of them, when addressing complaints filed against licensed practitioners, whether or not the practitioner is a member of the professional association that sponsors the relevant code. Also, a number of national and international organizations have developed guidelines for behavioral health professionals who offer distance counseling services—for example, the Association of Social Work Boards, American Telemedicine Association, International Society for Mental Health Online, and the Online Therapy Institute.

4. Review relevant regulations, laws, and policies. Behavioral health professionals who make difficult judgments that have legal implications should always consider relevant federal, state, and local regulations and laws. Many regulations and laws have direct relevance to practitioners' use of digital and distance technology; prominent examples concern the confidentiality of substance use disorder treatment records, the confidentiality of students' educational records, and the confidentiality of health care and mental health treatment records. A number of states have adopted laws and regulations that explicitly govern behavioral health professionals' provision of distance counseling services (for example, requiring practitioners to have a license in the client's state of residence, even if the practitioners live elsewhere).

In addition to state laws, key federal laws may be relevant to behavioral health professionals' use of digital and distance technology (such as HIPAA: Health Insurance Portability and Accountability Act; Title 42 CFR Part 2: Confidentiality of Substance Use Disorder Patient Records; and FERPA: The Family Educational Rights and Privacy Act). Title 42 CFR Part 2 includes strict regulations designed to protect client records created by federally funded programs for the treatment of substance use disorders (SUD). These regulations are much stricter than those included under HIPAA. One of the most important differences between 42 CFR Part 2 and HIPAA is the privacy protections for client records in criminal and civil legal proceedings. Part 2 regulations require a specific court order for the disclosure of Part 2-protected information in response to a subpoena, search warrant, or law enforcement request in conjunction with investigation of a crime. HIPAA permits disclosures without client consent that are not permitted under 42 CFR Part 2. These guidelines apply to behavioral health professionals who provide services remotely and who maintain electronic records.

Practitioners employed in school settings, including those who provide behavioral health services to students remotely (for example, during public health or other emergencies or when practitioners serve students enrolled in online school programs), must comply with FERPA. FERPA was enacted by Congress to protect the privacy of students and their parents. The act is designed to ensure that students and parents of students may obtain access to the student's educational records and challenge the content or release of such records to third parties. FERPA requires that federally funded institutions, under programs administered by the U.S. Department of Education, comply with certain procedures with regard to disclosing and maintaining educational records.

School-based behavioral health professionals who use technology to deliver services and maintain records must understand the ways in which they can legitimately protect their counseling records from disclosure. Not all the information collected and maintained by school-based clinicians is subject to the access and disclosure requirements under FERPA. One of the categories exempt from the definition of "education records" under FERPA is records made by teachers, supervisors, school counselors, administrators, and other school personnel that are kept in the sole possession of the maker of the record and are not accessible or revealed to any other person except a temporary substitute for the maker of the record. A sole-possession record is a memory jogger note, not official case records, and only memory joggers fall under sole-possession records. This would include sole possession records maintained by practitioners electronically.

5. Develop a social media policy for clients and staffers. Behavioral health professionals who consider engaging with clients electronically and providing clients with distance services would do well to develop a social media policy that they share with clients. Discussing these issues with clients at the beginning of the working relationship can help avoid boundary confusion and confidentiality breaches. Social media policies inform clients about how the practitioner manages use of online social networking sites, email, text messages, and online searches, focusing especially on relevant informed consent, privacy, confidentiality, and boundary issues. Typical social media policies include statements such as:

- This document outlines my office policies related to use of social media. Please read it to understand how I conduct myself on the Internet and how you can expect me to respond to various interactions that may occur between us on the Internet.

- I do not accept friend or contact requests from current or former clients on any social networking site (Facebook, LinkedIn, etc.). I believe that adding clients as friends or contacts on these sites can compromise your confidentiality and our respective privacy. It may also blur the boundaries of our professional-client relationship. Please let me know if you have questions about this.

- Please do not contact me by text message, unless it is only to schedule or reschedule an appointment. Text communications may not be secure, and I may not read these messages in a timely fashion. Also, any text communications may become a part of your legal medical record and will need to be documented in your chart. If you need to contact me between sessions, the best way to do so is by phone or by using secure telehealth software applications.

- Ordinarily, I will not search for information about you on Google, Facebook, or other search engines. I want to respect your privacy. I will only conduct an online search to find you or to check your recent status updates if I am concerned about your safety and you have not been in touch with me via our usual means (coming to appointments, phone, or email). These are unusual situations and if I ever resort to such means, I will fully document my online search and, when possible, will discuss it with you.

- I prefer using email only to arrange or modify appointments. Please do not email me content related to the work we do together, as email is not completely secure or confidential. If you choose to communicate with me by email, be aware that all emails are retained in the logs of your and my Internet service providers. While it is unlikely that someone will be looking at these logs, they are, in theory, available to be read by the system administrator(s) of the Internet service provider. You should also know that any emails I receive from you and any responses that I send to you become a part of your legal record.[1]

Behavioral health practitioners are quickly discovering that a comprehensive social media policy reflecting current ethical standards can simultaneously protect clients and practitioners.

Many behavioral health agencies have developed policies for employees outlining what is and is not permitted conduct with regard to their use of digital technology. Typical agency policies address employees' online interactions with clients and former clients, use of social networking sites (for example, Facebook, LinkedIn), email and text message communications, and personal blogs.

6. Review relevant literature. Behavioral health professionals should always keep current with professional literature pertaining to their use of digital and distance technology. When faced with challenging decisions, practitioners should make every reasonable effort to consult pertinent literature in an effort to determine what authorities in the field say about the issues. Such consultation can provide useful guidance and also provides helpful evidence that a practitioner made a conscientious attempt to comply with current standards in the field. That a practitioner took the time to consult pertinent literature "looks good," as a defense lawyer might say. In addition, practitioners can expect that opposing lawyers will conduct their own comprehensive review of relevant literature in an effort to locate authoritative publications that support their clients' claims. Lawyers often submit as evidence copies of publications that, in their opinion, buttress their legal case. Lawyers may use the authors of influential publications as expert witnesses.

7. Obtain legal consultation when necessary. Behavioral health professionals who consider using digital and distance technology would do well to consult with a health care attorney who is familiar with relevant laws and regulations. Ideally, practitioners who need legal advice related to their use of technology should consult with an attorney who has extensive experience defending practitioners who are named in lawsuits and licensing board complaints; typically, these attorneys are especially attuned to sound risk management strategies. In this emerging area of the law, statutes, regulations, and court decisions may address, for example, authorization to practice, confidentiality protections and exceptions, privileged communication, informed consent, documentation, conflicts of interest, and termination of services

---

1   This list draws on suggestions provided by Kolmes (2010).

(Saltzman, Furman, & Ohman, 2016). In addition, the fact that a practitioner took the time to obtain legal consultation provides additional evidence of having made conscientious, diligent efforts to use digital and distance technology responsibly.

8. Document decision-making steps. Comprehensive records are necessary to ensure documentation of practitioners' proper use of digital and distance technology to assess clients' circumstances; plan and deliver services; facilitate supervision; be accountable to clients, other service providers, funding agencies, insurers, utilization review staff, and the courts; evaluate services provided; and ensure continuity in the delivery of future services (Kagle & Kopels, 2008; Sidell, 2015). Thorough documentation also helps to ensure quality care if a client's primary clinician becomes unavailable because of illness, incapacitation, vacation, or employment termination; colleagues who provide coverage will have the benefit of up-to-date information.

In addition, thorough documentation can help protect practitioners who are named in ethics complaints and lawsuits (for example, documentation that a practitioner obtained consultation; consulted relevant literature and ethical and practice standards related to use of technology; referred a high-risk client for specialized services; obtained a client's informed consent for release of confidential information; or managed a client's suicide risk competently).

Careful and skilled documentation can protect clients and prevent ethics complaints and lawsuits. Electronic records associated with the delivery of online and distance services typically include:

- a complete social history, assessment, and treatment plan that states the client's problems, reason(s) for requesting services, objectives and relevant timetable, intervention strategy, planned number and duration of contacts, methods for assessment and evaluation of progress, termination plan, and reasons for termination;

- informed consent procedures, with particular attention to benefits and risks associated with online and distance services, and signed consent forms for treatment and release of information;

- notes on all contacts made with the client and third parties (such as family members, acquaintances, and other professionals)—whether in person, by telephone, or digital or online technology—including a brief description of the contacts and any important events surrounding them;

- notes on any consultation with other professionals, including the date the client was referred to another professional for service;

- a brief description of the practitioner's reasoning for all decisions made and interventions provided during the course of services;

- information summarizing any critical incidents (for example, suicide attempts, threats made by the client toward third parties, child abuse, family crises, technology failures) and the practitioner's response;

- any instructions, recommendations, and advice provided to the client, including referral to and suggestions to seek consultation from specialists (including physicians);

- notation of failed or canceled online or distance appointments;

- summaries of previous or current psychological, psychiatric, or medical evaluations relevant to the practitioner's intervention;

- information about fees, charges, and payment;

- reasons for termination and final assessment; and

- copies of all relevant documents, such as signed consent forms, correspondence, fee agreements, and court documents.

When behavioral health professionals document in electronic records, they should pay particular attention to the content of their documentation; the language and terminology they use; the credibility of their documentation; and policies related to third parties' access to records. Too much content, too little content, or the wrong content in electronic records can harm clients and expose practitioners to considerable risk of liability.

To ensure appropriate content in documentation, practitioners should consider several issues. A primary function of documentation is to serve and protect all parties. The content, however, must tread a careful line, striking a balance between too much and too little information. In a crisis situation, practitioners need to observe some precautions when recording case information. Including excessive detail in an electronic case record in the context of a crisis can serve as a "red flag" when records are reviewed during an ethics hearing or litigation.

Behavioral health professionals should include sufficient detail to facilitate the delivery of services and protect themselves in the event of an ethics complaint or lawsuit. Documenting too much or too little can be perilous. For example, in clinical settings too little detail about a client's suicidal ideation may compromise the quality of services provided by an on-call colleague who reviews incomplete or vague entries in the client's electronic record. Furthermore, practitioners who do not include sufficient detail concerning the steps they took to address a client's crisis are likely to have difficulty defending their actions in the event of an ethics complaint or negligence lawsuit.

In contrast, too much detail—a client's fantasies, for instance—could be used against the client if that client's spouse subpoenas the electronic record as part of a child custody dispute. Admittedly, distinguishing between too much and too little detail can be difficult. It requires experience and reasoned decision-making. Practitioners should strive for a reasonable balance considering what information is essential to properly assess clients' needs; plan, coordinate, deliver, supervise, and evaluate services; and be accountable to clients, insurers, agencies, other providers, courts, and utilization review bodies.

Wording in documentation is just as important as the substance of the content. Loose and casual language and terminology can be catastrophic. Practitioners must choose their words carefully, taking care to be clear, to fully support conclusions drawn, to avoid defamatory language, and to write knowing there is always an audience. Practitioners should use clear, specific, unambiguous, and precise wording. Lack of clarity, specificity, and precision provides considerable opportunity for adversarial parties to raise doubts about practitioners' claims, observations, and interpretations. In addition, these shortcomings in a report may confuse colleagues who are depending on the notes to provide follow-up services to clients.

Conversely, clear, specific, unambiguous, and precise wording enhances the delivery of services and strengthens practitioners' ability to explain and defend prior decisions and actions. In addition to using precise wording, practitioners should avoid the use of professional jargon, slang, or abbreviations that may be misunderstood. Such ambiguity could prove disastrous if the abbreviations are misinterpreted by a colleague or debated in an ethics hearing, licensing board inquiry, or litigation. Some electronic records software provides practitioners with a list of approved abbreviations.

It is very risky to document conclusions with terms or phrases such as "the client was confused" or "the unit counselor behaved aggressively toward the client" without including supporting details. Practitioners need to always include explanatory details that support a conclusion or assertion. Summary statements about the mental health status or behavior of a client, employee, or colleague should always be supported with sufficient details. Terms such as "hostile," "under the influence," or "incompetent" should always be reinforced and followed by the phrase "as evidenced by ..." with appropriate details included.

Practitioners should expect electronic records to be reviewed by managed care authorities, utilization review personnel, and third-party payers. Poorly worded and inadequate documentation may affect the likelihood that payment will be authorized for services to clients. Also, practitioners should protect clients' privacy when they share records with such outside parties, consistent with relevant ethical standards, laws, and agency policies.

Practitioners should enter their electronic notes in a timely fashion. Delayed documentation can compromise the credibility of practitioners' claims about what is reflected in the notes. Adversarial parties in a lawsuit, especially opposing legal counsel, can use evidence of delayed documentation to challenge the credibility of practitioners' testimony.

If practitioners discover an error in their electronic entry, they should acknowledge and correct the error forthrightly. Practitioners should never attempt to "cover up" or camouflage their errors. Such efforts can backfire. For example, opposing lawyers can access documents before practitioners attempt to conceal the errors. Lawyers may accuse practitioners who alter records of engaging in what is known as spoliation. Spoliation is the destruction or alteration of a document that destroys its value as evidence in a legal proceeding. Spoliation often carries an inference of intentional destruction in order to avoid negative implications associated with evidence. Behavioral health professionals who alter records in anticipation of legal proceedings, or after legal proceedings have been initiated, therefore, assume great risk and public humiliation if the inconsistencies are brought to light. Some electronic record software does not permit practitioners to delete prior entries. When warranted, practitioners should amend and correct an incorrect note.

Behavioral health practitioners who provide online and distance services should ensure that they have adequate insurance coverage. In addition to standard malpractice insurance, practitioners should strongly consider obtaining cyber liability coverage, which typically includes protection against inadvertent disclosure of confidential electronic data and other data breaches. Typical policies cover legal defense costs, state and federal fines and penalties, damages, audits conducted by computer security breach experts, client notification costs, and identification protection subscriptions for clients and victims.

CONCLUSION

Behavioral health has been transformed by the emergence of digital and other electronic technology. Most contemporary practitioners completed their formal education and entered their profession before currently available technology was invented, at a time when relationships with clients were limited to ongoing face-to-face meetings and the in-person development of a therapeutic alliance. In contrast, today's practitioners have the capacity to serve clients they never meet in person. Behavioral health educators can teach students who never set foot in a physical classroom. Supervisors can provide oversight remotely.

Also, practitioners are using technology to communicate with clients using text messaging and email, often for clinical purposes. Further, practitioners now are navigating boundary issues related to clients' and practitioners' use of online social networking sites and electronic search engines. And, practitioners in integrated health settings are managing complex confidentiality issues pertaining to staffers' access to sensitive information about clients stored in electronic records.

For some behavioral health professionals and clients, traditional office-based services have become an anachronism; the boundaries of the practitioner-client relationship are now much less clear and much more fluid and ambiguous. Contemporary practitioners must make thoughtful decisions about whether and to what extent they will incorporate digital and other electronic technology into their professional lives. They must reflect on the meaning and nature of the professional-client relationship, and the ways in which digital technology enhances or detracts from it. Practitioners' judgments should draw on prevailing ethical standards and standards of care. Behavioral health professionals should keep in mind that this is a rapidly developing component of professional practice, one in which ethical and risk management standards will continue to evolve.

References

Alden, J. (2020, March 11). *Health care group hit with California privacy law breach suit.* Bloomberg Law. https://news.bloomberglaw.com /privacy-and-data-security/health-care-group-hit-with-california-privacy-law-breach-suit

American Association for Marriage and Family Therapy. (2015). *Code of ethics.* https://www.aamft.org/Legal_Ethics/Code_of_Ethics.aspx

American Counseling Association. (2014). *ACA code of ethics.* https:// www.counseling.org/docs/default-source/default-document-library/2014-code-of-ethics-finaladdress.pdf?sfvrsn=96b532c_2

American Psychiatric Association. (2020). *Telepsychiatry.* https://www. psychiatry.org/psychiatrists/practice/telepsychiatry

American Psychological Association. (2017). *Ethical principles of psychologists and code of conduct.* https://www.apa.org/ethics/ code/?item=6#310

American Psychological Association. (2020). *Guidelines for the practice of telepsychology.* https://www.apa.org/practice/guidelines/ telepsychology

Anderson, S. C., & Guyton, M. R. (2013). Ethics in an age of information seekers: A survey of licensed healthcare providers about online social networking. *Journal of Technology in Human Services, 31,* 112–128.

Andersson, G. (2016). Internet-delivered psychological treatments. *Annual Review of Clinical Psychology, 12,* 157–179.

Association of Marital and Family Therapy Regulatory Boards. (2016). *Teletherapy guidelines.* https://amftrb.org/wp-content/uploads/2017/05/ Proposed-Teletherapy-Guidelines-DRAFT-as-of-09.12.16.pdf

Association of Social Work Boards. (2015). *Model regulatory standards for technology and social work practice.* https://www.aswb. org/wp-content/uploads/2015/03/ASWB-Model-Regulatory-Standards-for-Technology-and-Social-Work-Practice.pdf

Banks, S. (2012). *Ethics and values in social work* (4th ed.). Palgrave Macmillan.

Barak, A., & Grohol, J. M. (2011). Current and future trends in Internet-supported mental health interventions. *Journal of Technology in Human Services, 29,* 155–196.

Barak, A., Hen, L., Boniel-Nissim, M., & Shapira, N. (2008). A comprehensive review and a meta-analysis of the effectiveness of Internet-based psycho-therapeutic interventions. *Journal of Technology in Human Services, 26,* 109–160.

Barsky, A. (2017). Social work practice and technology: Ethical issues and policy responses. *Journal of Technology in Human Services, 35,* 8–19.

Barsky, A. (2019). *Ethics and values in the social work profession* (2nd ed.). Oxford University Press.

Bashshur, R., Shannon, G., Bashshur, N., & Yellowlees, P. (2016). The empirical evidence for telemedicine interventions in mental disorders. *Telemedicine and e-Health, 22,* 87–113.

Bentley, K. J., Secret, M. C., & Cummings, C. R. (2015). The centrality of social presence in online teaching and learning in social work. *Journal of Social Work Education, 5,* 494–504.

Berg, J. W., Appelbaum, P. S., Lidz, C. W., & Parker, L. S. (2001). *Informed consent: Legal theory and clinical practice* (2nd ed.). Oxford University Press.

Berle, D., Starcevic, V., Milicevic, D., Hannan, A., Dale, E., Brakoulias, V., & Viswasam, K. (2015). Do patients prefer face-to-face or internet-based therapy? *Psychotherapy and Psychosomatics, 84,* 61–62.

Bernstein, B., & Hartsell, T. (2004). *The portable lawyer for mental health professionals* (2nd ed.). Wiley.

Boettcher, J. V., & Conrad, R. (2016). *The online teaching survival guide: Simple and practical pedagogical tips* (2nd ed.). Jossey-Bass.

Brownlee, K. (1996). The ethics of nonsexual dual relationships: A dilemma for the rural mental health professional. *Community Mental Health Journal, 32,* 497–503.

Campbell, C. D., & Gordon, M. C. (2003). Acknowledging the inevitable: Understanding multiple relationships in rural practice. *Professional Psychology: Research and Practice, 34,* 430–434.

Campbell, L., Millan, F., & Martin, J. (Eds.). (2018). *A telepsychology casebook: Using technology ethically and effectively in your professional practice.* American Psychological Association.

Carroll, R. A. (Ed.). (2011). *Risk management handbook for healthcare organizations* (6th ed.). Wiley.

Chaffin, C. (2019, June 25). *More than 645,000 Oregonians impacted by DHS data breach.* The Oregonian. https://www.oregonlive.com/data/2019/06/more-than-645000-oregonians-impacted-by-dhs-data-breach.html

Chan, C., & Holosko, M. (2016). A review of information and communication technology enhanced social work interventions. *Research on Social Work Practice, 26,* 88–100.

Chang, T. (2005). Online counseling: Prioritizing psychoeducation, self-help, and mutual help for counseling psychology research and practice. *Counseling Psychologist, 33,* 881–890.

Chester, A., & Glass, C. A. (2006). Online counseling: A descriptive analysis of therapy services on the internet. *British Journal of Guidance and Counseling, 34,* 145–160.

Clinton, B. K., Silverman, B., & Brendel, D. (2010). Patient-targeted Googling: The ethics of searching online for patient information. *Harvard Review of Psychiatry, 18,* 103–112.

Collins, C., Hewson, D., Munger, R., & Wade, T. (2010). *Evolving models of behavioral health integration in primary care.* Milbank Memorial Fund.

Cooper, M. G., & Lesser, J. G. (2010). *Clinical social work* (4th ed.). Allyn and Bacon.

Corey, G., Corey, M. S., & Corey, C. (2019). *Issues and ethics in the helping professions* (10th ed.). Cengage.

Council on Social Work Education. (2015). *Educational policy and accreditation standards.* https://www.cswe.org/Accreditation/Standards-and-Policies/2015-EPAS.aspx

Curtis, R., & Christian, E. (2012). *Integrated care: Applying theory to practice.* Routledge.

Daley, M., & Doughty, M. (2006). Ethics complaints in social work practice: A rural–urban comparison. *Journal of Social Work Values and Ethics, 3*(1). http://jswve.org/download/2006-1/JSWVE-Spring-2006-Complete.pdf

Daviss, S., Hanson, A., & Miller, D. (2015). My three shrinks: Personal stories of social media exploration. *International Review of Psychiatry, 27,* 167–173.

Dixson, M. (2010). Creating effective student engagement in online courses: What do students find engaging? *Journal of the Scholarship of Teaching and Learning, 10,* 1–13.

Dombo, E., Kays, L., & Weller, K. (2014). Clinical social work practice and technology: Personal, practical, regulatory and ethical considerations for the twenty-first century. *Social Work in Health Care, 53,* 900–919.

Dowling, M., & Rickwood, D. (2013). Online counseling and therapy for mental health problems: A systematic review of individual synchronous interventions using chat. *Journal of Technology in Human Services, 31,* 1–21.

Duncan-Daston, R., Hunter-Sloan, M., & Fullmer, E. (2013). Considering the ethical implications of social media in social work education. *Ethics and Information Technology, 15,* 35–43.

Fange, L., Mishna, F., Zhang, V. F., Van Wert, M., & Bogo, M. (2014). Social media and social work education: Understanding and dealing with the new digital world. *Social Work in Health Care, 53,* 800–814.

Federal Trade Commission (2016, June 8). Electronic health records company settles FTC charges it deceived consumers about privacy of doctor reviews [Press release]. https://www.ftc.gov/news-events/press-releases/2016/06/electronic-health-records-company-settles-ftc-charges-it-deceived

Finn, J. (2006). An exploratory study of email use by direct service social workers. *Journal of Technology in Human Services, 24,* 1–20.

Finn, J., & Barak, A. (2010). A descriptive study of e-counsellor attitudes, ethics, and practice. *Counselling and Psychotherapy Review, 24*, 268–277.

Gabbard, G., Kassaw, G., & Perez-Garcia, G. (2011). Professional boundaries in the era of the Internet. *Academic Psychiatry, 35*, 168–174.

Glueckauf, R. L., Maheu, M. M., Drude, K. P., Wells, B. A., Wang, Y., Gustafson, D. J., & Nelson, E. (2018). Survey of psychologists' telebehavioral health practices: Technology use, ethical issues, and training needs. *Professional Psychology: Research and Practice, 49*, 205–219.

Goldingay, S., & Boddy, J. (2017). Preparing social work graduates for digital practice: Ethical pedagogies for effective learning. *Australian Social Work, 70*, 209–220.

Graffeo, I., & La Barbera, D. (2009). Cybertherapy meets Facebook, blogger, and second life: An Italian experience. *Annual Review of Cybertherapy and Telemedicine, 7*, 108–112.

Grant, G. B., & Grobman, L. M. (1998). *The social worker's Internet handbook*. White Hat Communications.

Greysen, S., Chretien, K., Kind, T., Young, A., & Gross, C. (2012). Physician violations of online professionalism and disciplinary actions: A national survey of state medical boards. *Journal of the American Medical Association, 307*, 1141–1142.

Grimm, P. W., Ziccardi, M. V., & Major, A. W. (2009). Back to the future: Lorraine v. Markel American Insurance Co. and new findings on the admissibility of electronically stored information. *Akron Law Review, 42*, 357–418.

Gross, A. (2019, April 30). *Misconfigured webpage exposed patient data*. HIPPA Secure Now. https://www.hipaasecurenow.com/index.php/category/business-associates/

Gupta, A., & Agrawal, A. (2012). Internet counselling and psychological services. *Social Science International, 28*, 105–122.

Gutheil, T. G., & Simon, R. (2005). Emails, extra-therapeutic contact, and early boundary problems: The Internet as a "slippery slope." *Psychiatric Annals, 35*, 952–960.

Haberstroh, S. (2009). Strategies and resources for conducting online counseling. *Journal of Professional Counseling: Practice, Theory and Research, 37*, 1–20.

Horevitz, E., & Manoleas, P. (2013). Professional competencies and training needs of professional social workers in integrated behavioral health in primary care. *Social Work in Health Care, 52*, 752–787.

Hu, J., Chen, H., & Hou, T. (2010). A hybrid public key infrastructure solution (HPKI) for HIPAA privacy/security regulations. *Computer Standards and Interfaces, 32*, 274–280.

Kagle, J. D., & Kopels, S. (2008). *Social work records* (2nd ed.). Waveland Press.

Kanani, K., & Regehr, C. (2003). Clinical, ethical, and legal issues in e-therapy. *Families in Society, 84*, 155–162.

Klein, C. (2011). Cloudy confidentiality: Clinical and legal implications of cloud computing in health care. *Journal of the American Academy of Psychiatry and the Law, 39,* 571–578.

Knapp, S., VandeCreek, L., & Fingerhut, R. (2017). *Practical ethics for psychologists: A positive approach* (3rd ed.). American Psychological Association.

Ko, S., & Rossen, S. (2017). *Teaching online: A practical guide.* Routledge.

Kolmes, K. (2010). Developing my private practice social media policy. *Independent Practitioner, 30,* 140–142.

Kolmes, K., & Taube, D. (2016). Client discovery of psychotherapist personal information online. *Professional Psychology: Research and Practice, 47,* 147–154.

Lakhani, A. (2013). Social networking sites and the legal profession: Balancing benefits with navigating minefields. *Computer Law & Security Review, 29,* 164–174.

Lamendola, W. (2010). Social work and social presence in an online world. *Journal of Technology in the Human Services, 28,* 108–119.

Lannin, D. G., & Scott, N. A. (2013). Social networking ethics: Developing best practices for the new small world. *Professional Psychology: Research and Practice, 44,* 135–141.

Lee, S. (2010). Contemporary issues of ethical e-therapy. *Frontline Perspectives, 5,* 1–5.

Lindeman, D. (2011). Interview: Lessons from a leader in telehealth diffusion: A conversation with Adam Darkins of the Veterans Health Administration. *Ageing International, 36,* 146–154.

Luxton, D., Nelson, E., & Maheu, M. (2016). *A practitioner's guide to telemental health: How to conduct legal, ethical, and evidence-based telepractice.* American Psychological Association.

MacDonald, J., Sohn, S., & Ellis, P. (2010). Privacy, professionalism and Facebook: A dilemma for young doctors. *Medical Education, 44,* 805–813.

Maidment, J. (2006). Using on-line delivery to support students during practicum placements. *Australian Social Work, 59,* 47–55.

Mallen, M. J., Jenkins, I. M., Vogel, D. L., & Day, S. X. (2011). Online counselling: An initial examination of the process in a synchronous chat environment. *Counselling and Psychotherapy Research, 11,* 220–227.

Martinez, R. C., & Clark, C. L. (2000). *The social worker's guide to the Internet.* Allyn & Bacon.

Mattison, M. (2012). Social work practice in the digital age: Therapeutic email as a direct practice methodology. *Social Work, 57,* 249–258.

McCarty, D., & Clancy, C. (2002). Telehealth: Implications for social work practice. *Social Work, 47,* 153–161.

Menon, G. M., & Miller-Cribbs, J. (2002). Online social work practice: Issues and guidelines for the profession. *Advances in Social Work, 3,* 104–116.

Midkiff, D., & Wyatt, W. J. (2008). Ethical issues in the provision of online mental health services (etherapy). *Technology in Human Services, 26,* 310–332.

Morgan, S., & Polowy, C. (2011). *Social workers and Skype: Part I. NASW Legal Defense Fund, Legal Issue of the Month.* https://www.naswal.org/page/70

National Association of Social Workers. (2017). *National Association of Social Workers Code of Ethics.* https://www.socialworkers.org/About/Ethics/Code-of-Ethics/Code-of-Ethics-English

National Association of Social Workers, Association of Social Work Boards, Council on Social Work Education, & Clinical Social Work Association. (2017). *Standards for technology in social work practice.* National Association of Social Workers.

National Board for Certified Counselors. (2016a). *Code of ethics.* https://www.nbcc.org/Assets/Ethics/NBCCCodeofEthics.pdf

National Board for Certified Counselors. (2016b). *National Board for Certified Counselors policy regarding the provision of distance professional services.* https://www.nbcc.org/Assets/Ethics/NBCCPolicyRegardingPracticeofDistanceCounselingBoard.pdf

National Center on User Design for Learning. (2018). *The UDL guidelines.* http://udlguidelines.cast.org/

Peterson, M. R., & Beck, R. L. (2003). Email as an adjunctive tool in psychotherapy: Response and responsibility. *American Journal of Psychotherapy, 51,* 167–181.

Phelan, J. (2015). The use of e-learning in social work education. *Social Work, 60,* 257–264.

Reamer, F. G. (2012a). The digital and electronic revolution in social work: Rethinking the meaning of ethical practice. *Ethics and Social Welfare, 7,* 2–19.

Reamer, F. G. (2012b). *Boundary issues and dual relationships in the human services.* Columbia University Press.

Reamer, F. G. (2013a). Social work in a digital age: Ethical and risk management challenges. *Social Work, 58,* 163–172.

Reamer, F. G. (2013b). Distance and online social work education: Novel ethical challenges. *Journal of Teaching in Social Work, 33*(4–5), 369–384.

Reamer, F. G. (2015). Clinical social work in a digital environment: Ethical and risk-management challenges. *Clinical Social Work Journal, 43,* 120–132.

Reamer, F. G. (2017). Evolving ethical standards in the digital age. *Australian Social Work, 70,* 148–159.

Reamer, F. G. (2018a). Ethical standards for social workers' use of technology: Emerging consensus. *Journal of Social Work Values and Ethics, 15,* 71–80.

Reamer, F. G. (2018b). Evolving standards of care in the age of cybertechnology. *Behavioral Sciences and the Law, 36,* 257–269.

Reamer, F. G. (2018c). *Social work values and ethics* (5th ed.). Columbia University Press.

Reamer, F. G. (2018d). *Ethical standards in social work: A review of the NASW code of ethics* (3rd ed.). NASW Press.

Reamer, F. G. (2018e). *The social work ethics casebook: Cases and commentary* (2nd ed.). NASW Press.

Reamer, F. G. (2018f). Ethical issues in integrated health care: Implications for social workers. *Health and Social Work, 43,* 118–124.

Reamer, F. G. (2019). Social work education in a digital world: Technology standards for education and practice. *Journal of Social Work Education, 55,* 420–432.

Recupero, P., & Rainey, S. E. (2005). Forensic aspects of e-therapy. *Journal of Psychiatric Practice, 11,* 405–410.

Recupero, P., & Reamer, F. (2018). The internet and forensic ethics. In E. Griffith (Ed.), *Ethics challenges in forensic psychiatry and psychology practice* (pp. 208–222). Columbia University Press.

Reeves, P. M., & Reeves, T. C. (2008). Design considerations for online learning in health and social work education. *Learning in Health and Social Care, 7,* 46–58.

Richards, D., & Vigano, N. (2013). Online counseling: A narrative and critical review of the literature. *Journal of Clinical Psychology, 69,* 994–1011.

Rummell, C. M., & Joyce, N. R. (2010). "So wat do u want to wrk on 2 day?": The ethical implications of online counselling. *Ethics and Behavior, 20,* 482–496.

Saltzman, A., Furman, D., & Ohman, K. (2016). *Law in social work practice* (3rd ed.). Cengage.

Santhiveeran, J. (2009). Compliance of social work e-therapy websites to the NASW code of ethics. *Social Work in Health Care, 48,* 1–13.

Sawrikar, P., Lenette, C., McDonald, D., & Fowler, J. (2015). Don't silence the dinosaurs: Keeping caution alive with regard to social work distance education. *Journal of Teaching in Social Work, 35,* 343–364.

Schoech, D. (1999). *Human services technology: Understanding, designing, and implementing computer and Internet applications in social services.* Haworth Press.

Shore, J. (2015). The evolution and history of telepsychiatry and its impact on psychiatric care: Current implications for psychiatrists and psychiatric organizations. *International Review of Psychiatry, 27,* 469–475.

Sidell, N. L. (2015). *Social work documentation: A guide to strengthening your case recording* (2nd ed.). NASW Press.

Siebert, D., Siebert, C., & Spaulding-Givens, J. (2013). Teaching clinical social work skills primarily online: An evaluation. *Journal of Social Work Education, 42,* 325–336.

Siegler, E., & Adelman, R. (2009). Copy and paste: A remediable hazard of electronic health records. *American Journal of Medicine, 122,* 495–496.

Skinner, A., & Zack, J. S. (2004). Counseling and the internet. *American Behavioral Scientist, 48,* 434–446.

Stevenson, L. (2014, September 10). *HCPC sanctions social worker over Facebook posts.* Community Care. https://www.communitycare.co.uk/2014/09/10/social-work-er-given-conditions-practice-order-disrespectful-facebook-posts/

Sukel, K. (2019, May 23). *Is your EHR a malpractice risk?* Medical Economics. https://www.medicaleconomics.com/news/your-ehr-malpractice-risk

Sulmasy, L., Lopez, A., Horwitch, C., & American College of Physicians Ethics, Professionalism, and Human Rights Committee. (2017). Ethical implications of the electronic health record: In the service of the patient. *Journal of General Internal Medicine, 32*, 935–939.

Telehealth Resource Center. (2020). Cross-state licensure. https://www.telehealthresourcecenter.org/knowledgebase_category/cross-state-licensure/

Zur, O. (2007). *Boundaries in psychotherapy: Ethical and clinical explorations.* American Psychological Association.

Zur, O. (2012). TelePsychology or TeleMentalHealth in the digital age: The future is here. *California Psychologist, 45*, 13–15.

Index